Bonnie & Clyde – May 23, 1934
Retribution
Allison Bateman

ISBN-13: 978-1515040453
ISBN-10: 1515040453

Contents

Introduction

In the end, Bonnie and Clyde became the most famous outlaws America has ever known. They killed and robbed, but the public, which was suffering through a wrenching depression, picked up their trail and made them into folk heroes. Then the law, through actions reminiscent of the old west, formed a posse and prepared to ambush them. The law, and the violent end, which led to their deaths, immortalized them, and they became legends.

Speculation on the couple ran unchecked, and then Hollywood took over. Today, Bonnie and Clyde are larger than life. The public cannot seem to get enough of these two famous folk heroes.

The nation's attention was focused on Bonnie as they tried to figure out what role she played. The only warrant issued for her arrest was helping to transport a stolen car across state lines. When Bonnie was gunned down, there were no active warrants for her arrest. The law had no evidence that she ever fired a gun at anyone. Today, historians continue to discuss whether she even knew how to shoot one. There was no evidence that she stole anything, as Bonnie always paid for items she wanted. That raises a serious question, was Bonnie's death, a cold-blooded murder.

Bonnie and Clyde started life as ordinary people, but because of the Great Depression, their lives took a turn for the worst. They became involved in small-time robberies, which quickly led to murder. While not condoning what they did, one has to admire their boldness and their willingness to ride it out to the end, even if it meant death to both of them. They have been dead for more than three-quarters of a century, but finally, they have come full circle.

Bonnie Parker, in her short life, had a fascination with the outlaws of the old west. She read stories about Billy the Kid, the Dalton Gang, and Bill Cook. However, it was the James Younger Gang that she had the most interest in. She would also have been aware of "the dirty little coward," Bob Ford. He shot Jesse James in the back, for the promise of a full pardon and reward money.

In the two-year heyday of Bonnie and Clyde, the two would have travelled across thousands of miles, as they continuously crisscrossed six states in the American mid-south. During all those miles on long lonely roads, would Bonnie have told Clyde, the story about Jesse James? More importantly, would she have mentioned the story about Bob Ford?

If Clyde was listening, then he failed to understand that outlaw gangs do produce traitors. These traitors will kill their leader for money and a clean slate. Just like in Jesse James, the lead person of the Barrow gang was killed by a traitor on the inside. Unfortunately, Bonnie was always with Clyde, and therefore, she was a marked woman. The other question is, would Bonnie have understood the following. As their time grew shorter, it would become more probable that some remaining members of the gang could double-cross them. And that is precisely what happened.

Notice:

The era of Bonnie and Clyde attracted a lot of public attention, and to many people, they became folk heroes. Because of the vast interest in these two famous outlaws, much has been written about them. There is everything from long-winded books to short stories, songs, and movies. Even people that were directly involved are accused of sugar coating the facts. Thus, it has become impossible to separate some facts from fiction. A lot of their history has become romanticized, but I guess that is what makes the legend so enduring.

Chapter 1
Bonnie Parker

If Bonnie Parker had been born in another place at another time, she could have had a successful career. She may have chosen a career in sales and marketing, promotions or even business development. She proved to the world in a short time that she had a talent for lifting herself into the category of a folk hero.

Bonnie was no giant as an adult, she weighed 90 pounds wringing wet and stood four' 11" in her bare feet. In grade school, she excelled, showing a talent for poetry and creative writing. She was at the top of her class in mathematics and spelling. Bonnie was never given an IQ test, but many believed her IQ was above average.

The question then arises, how could such a smart young woman get so far-off the beaten path that she could not find her way back? The answer to that was a combination of several events. Her father died when she was four years old, and her mother had to raise three children by herself. She did this in the deepest days during the depression in a suburb of Dallas, called Cement City, which had a high crime rate.

Bonnie's grandparents lived there. There was no money, no jobs, and the future for a bright and beautiful woman like Bonnie was desolate for sure. Bonnie married at age sixteen, too young, and her husband was unstable and involved in crime. Bonnie dumped him when she was eighteen, and then had to work as a waitress to support herself. However, she lost that job when the business closed.

She then accepted a job as a housekeeper, and it was there she met Clyde Barrow. Clyde soon started paying attention to her, and Bonnie became entangled in a life of crime. In a few short years, the two of them would become America's most-wanted criminals. Ironically, the American public would become fascinated by their adventures.

Bonnie, as a young child, was compared to Shirley Temple. This comparison originated in the 1940s. She had strawberry-blonde hair with a freckled face. She was born on October 1, 1910, in Rowena, Texas. Her full birth name was Bonnie Elizabeth Parker, and her father was Charles Parker, a bricklayer by trade. Her mother was Emma Krause Parker, and she was a seamstress. Bonnie had one older brother Hubert and a younger sister Billie Jean.

In school, Bonnie always felt sorry for the less fortunate, and she would help those students. This was a natural trait, which she carried over into her adult life. It became so obvious when she started hanging around with Clyde Barrow, and the two became inseparable.

As a young teenager Bonnie loved music, especially Jimmy Rogers, she loved all kinds of hats, and her favourite colour was red. Whenever she could afford it, she wore fashionable clothes dominated by that colour.

Bonnie was confident and outgoing, and she could turn heads. At one point, she wrote in her diary that she felt trapped in a place where nothing ever happened. She was perceptive, "because in those days," there were limited opportunities in West Dallas.

In an attempt to make something happen, she married Ray Thornton at the age of sixteen. Within a year, she realized that it was a big mistake. Thornton was convicted of murder and sent off to prison. Bonnie never spoke much about him after that, but she also never divorced him.

Bonnie developed an interest in the outlaws of the old west, while in school. She also had an interest in the Battle of the Little Big Horn, which was a bit unusual for a young woman. Many believe Bonnie had extrasensory perception. That was obvious when she wrote a poem about her and Clyde being taken down by the law. Some people thought that was inevitable.

Bonnie was fascinated by the horse that survivor of the Battle of the Little Big Horn. She was intrigued to find out the horse, whose name was Comanche, became a national celebrity. In death, his status soared as he became the most famous horse in the world. Bonnie's teachers said, "She was in total awe, to find out the U.S. Government buried Comanche with full military honours.

Bonnie did not have the best outlook on life, but one can forgive her for that. Her attitude probably reflects the grinding poverty she was subject to in West Dallas as a child. Girls from, what was known as Cement City were regulated to meaningless jobs. The horrors and degradations automatically came with these jobs. In 1933, Bonnie's sister, Billie Jean, lost both of her children to illness. Typhoid and pneumonia ran rampant in West Dallas, and many dirt-poor families lost their children. It's hard to say if Bonnie came to terms with the deaths of her niece and nephew, and that probably weighed on her decision to run with the wild bunch.

Male gangsters during that period in time dominated the scene. Clyde's partner was a beautiful female, and she had a flair for taking pictures of them together. Bonnie also wrote poetry and short stories about their exploits. She promoted the two of them, and it was not long before the public was following their adventures. Bonnie and Clyde did not fall under the gangster category. They were outlaws, fashioned more like the outlaws of the old American West. Bonnie was no stranger to the outlaws, and she patterned their adventures after Jessie James.

For Bonnie, the good life wasn't meant to be. She was destined to fulfil a unique role, one where she would lose her life violently. In the end, her life and legend would make her a folk hero. Bonnie Parker died at the age of 23, on a lonely stretch of road in Louisiana on May 23, 1934.

Chapter 2

Clyde Barrow

Clyde Chestnut Barrow was born on March 24, 1909, on a small farm outside Texas. He was the fifth of seven children from a poor farming family that moved to Dallas in 1922. Their new home was primarily a tent with garbage piled everywhere and open running sewers. For the first six months, the Barrow family lived under their wagon. Finally, the father, Henry, earned enough money to buy a tent, and the family moved into it.

Clyde was moved around in his childhood, and this created neglect and antisocial behaviour in him. Clyde's first arrest was for auto theft, and he was charged. That brush with the law did nothing to change his outlook on life. He committed a series of robberies in the Dallas area over the next four years and was moved around to different family members. His brother Buck helped him with some of those robberies. In 1930, his luck ran out when he was sent to the Eastham Prison Farm. It was here that Clyde hardened after he was raped several times by a dominant prisoner. Finally, Clyde struck back and hit the fellow over the head with a steel pipe. That was his first killing.

Clyde Chestnut Barrow became a national celebrity, but his size was less than impressive. He weighed 130 pounds, and he stood 5' 7" tall. He had brown eyes and brown hair, which he wore slicked back, the style for those days. Like Bonnie, his parents were dirt-poor. He was born into a life of poverty, something we can't hold against him.

In February 1932, Clyde was paroled and walked out of Eastham, a hardened and bitter person. Clyde's sister Nell noticed right away that he was different. He had a sour attitude, and she believed he would continue to break the law.

He started his criminal career almost immediately, and this time it was a full-time job. His work consisted of robbing corner stores, gas stations and anything else that showed the promise of easy money.

However, unlike Bonnie, Clyde could have been born anywhere at any time, and he probably would not have amounted to much. He was a small-time thief, and without Bonnie, his exploits would have gone unnoticed by the public. He did meet Bonnie, and the two of them fought their way across six states over three years. They robbed small-town banks, corner stores and gas stations. Clyde was the cold-blooded killer as he became trigger-happy, whenever he felt threatened or boxed-in. He had a talent for being an excellent shot and had nine lives like a cat. He shot his way out of several situations where a lesser man would probably have been killed or captured.

Chapter 3

The Partnership, Forged by Love

There are several stories of how Bonnie and Clyde first met each other. Most historians believe Bonnie met Clyde in January 1930. Bonnie, after losing her job at a restaurant (closed for lack of customers), was staying in West Dallas to help out a girlfriend, who had a broken arm. As the story goes, Clyde dropped by the house and noticed Bonnie in the kitchen making hot chocolate. The relationship progressed from that point.

When they met, both were infatuated with the other. It is generally agreed that Bonnie joined Barrow because she was in love. As Clyde carried out his crime spree, Bonnie remained a loyal companion to him. No doubt, they both knew it was only a matter of time until the law caught up with them.

In 1930, after meeting Bonnie, the police jailed Clyde for burglary in Waco. However, Bonnie could not stand the thought of being without him. She visited the jail, slipping a handgun past the guards. Clyde used the gun to escape, but was caught a week later in Ohio and sentenced to fourteen years of hard labour in the Texas State Pen. He was paroled in 1932 and became the infamous head of the Barrow Gang. Bonnie, a loyal companion, was with him every step of the way.

What did Bonnie have that made her the object of so much attention? What was her charm that struck a chord in the hearts of the American public? She was a female and a beautiful one at that, which gave her the advantage in an outlaw gangster world of men. If you take Bonnie out of the equation, Clyde was nothing more than a petty crook, who knocked off gas stations and small stores. Even with Bonnie, he never attempted to rob big banks. When you think about it, the two of them were wildly incompetent and made mistakes, which cost people their lives. Seasoned gangsters of that era often ridiculed Bonnie and Clyde for their amateur ways. One senior gangster came right out and said, the two of them gave bank robbing a bad name.

Chapter 4
The Joplin Hideout, The Turning Point
Early April 1933

When Eastham Prison released Clyde in February 1932, he wanted revenge for what the prison did to him. He planned to raid the prison, and release as many prisoners as possible. To carry this out, he wanted his brother Buck to back him up. Clyde contacted Buck, who was visiting with their mother, and he tried to persuade him to join in the effort. Buck's wife, Blanche, didn't want any part of it and wanted Buck to stay clear of Clyde. However, Buck convinced Blanch to go with him and meet his brother. The plan was to try to persuade Clyde, to give up his criminal life, and go straight.

Blanch agreed with the plan, but only after Buck told her he would return to Dallas regardless of the outcome and get a job. Buck purchased a Marmon (car) for the trip, and the two, with their dog Snowball, headed for a tourist camp in Checotah, Oklahoma.

They left on Tuesday, March 28, 1933. It was at this camp they were going to meet Bonnie, Clyde and Jones. The two couples would drive to Joplin, Missouri, where they would rent an apartment over a two-bay garage at 3347 Oak Ridge Drive.

The two-bedroom apartment came fully furnished, and the only item Clyde had to buy was a mattress for Jones. He would use this to sleep in the living room. When you're a criminal and running from the law, one does not carry many personal items around. Bonnie and Clyde only carried the bare supplies, plus a gun collection that would rival a small army platoon.

The five of them relaxed for a few days and spent their time cleaning guns, drinking, and playing cards. They also went for walks and took in the odd movie. Blanch and Buck tried a couple of times to talk Clyde into giving up his life of crime, but it was hopeless. Clyde was consumed with getting back at the Eastham Prison. His plan called for plenty of guns and money, which meant more robberies.

However, neighbours were becoming suspicious, and they reported their findings to the police. The police suspected an illegal bootlegging operation had set up. They scheduled a raid on the residents of the apartment for April 13, 1933. Little did they know who they were up against. The five residents, feeling uneasy about the calm, decided to leave the apartment on April 14, which would be one day too late.

On April 13, the two women spent the day packing their gear and cleaning the apartment. Buck began checking the cars to make sure everything was okay. Meanwhile, Clyde and Jones took the Ford sedan and went looking for some places to rob. The Barrow Gang was short on cash and needed some for their trip. They returned just after lunch with a fresh roll of bills.

By mid-afternoon, there were only minor chores to finish, and the party went over their final plans. Buck and Blanch were heading back to Texas, while Bonnie, Clyde and Jones were going on to Michigan. Clyde heard a noise at the front of the house, which sounded like a car. He walked into the living room to have a look at the street. There in the driveway was a cop car, and two lawmen were behind it with long-barrel guns. Clyde yelled to the rest of them, and the men grabbed their weapons. Bonnie quickly threw items into a bag. Clyde yelled at the women to get into the cars.

Clyde opened fire with a burst at the police. Jones also opened fire with Buck. Most of the front windows were shot out immediately. Clyde yelled, "Everyone in the sedan." Buck was the first down the stairs, and as he entered the garage, he opened fire on a lawman, who had entered the building. The officer fell and was dead before hitting the cement floor. By this time, the law outside was ducking, for they were being sprayed with automatic gunfire from several sources. They did not come prepared for this kind of a shootout. Clyde still upstairs, grabbed one of his special browning guns with a 45 round clip and let loose. All the lawmen outside took cover as Clyde sprayed the area with armour-piercing shells.

The weapon fire gave the others a chance to go downstairs and into the car. Jones then opened up with a second 45 round gun from the front door and continued spraying the area with deadly shells. The lawmen kept their heads down as doing anything else would have been suicide.

Buck and Blanche dove outside and began pushing the police car backwards. While they were pushing the car, Jones and Clyde continued spraying the area with shells. With the police car out-of-the-way, everyone jumped into the sedan. Bonnie handed Buck and Jones a full 45 round clip for each gun. Clyde hit the gas, and the Ford V8 took out the garage door and pulled onto the road. Buck and Jones continued to spray everything in sight with shells.

As the getaway car raced down the street and turned right onto main, the police emerged dazed and in disbelief to what had just happened. They quickly decided not to chase the gang, as they did not have the firepower to compete with these criminals, whoever they were. The officers rushed to two of their own, one lying on the driveway, and the other in the garage. Both men were dead. Four other officers had minor gunshot wounds. Three cop cars were shot-up, and one private car had taken several hits.

One officer remarked, "This will be a day that will go down in Joplin's history." One of the other officers remarked, "He saw at least one woman in the getaway car." He went on to say," I believe we just had a shootout.

with Bonnie and Clyde and the Barrow Gang."

The gang's Joplin, Missouri hideout was the beginning of the end for

Bonnie and Clyde. The gang made several crucial mistakes, which led to a shootout leaving two lawmen dead.

In looking at their mistakes, Bonnie left behind undeveloped rolls of film. When the police had them developed, several pictures were delivered to newspapers across the country. The public could now put faces to the Barrow gang. One of Bonnie's most famous pictures shows her toting a gun. In that picture, she was smoking a cigar with one foot on the front bumper of a car. That was a prank picture of Bonnie and was never intended for the public to see. Bonnie did not smoke cigars, and she went to great lengths to get that information out to the public, as she hated that picture of herself.

Bonnie left behind poetry, which was not harmful. She always made sure her diary was with her. That was sensible on her part, as there was damaging information written in it. The pictures and poems left behind revealed the now-famous images of Bonnie and Clyde. All this information, the guns and their escape from the law at Joplin added to their legend, making them even more famous.

While at the Joplin hideout, the gang acted suspicious, and this caught the eye of neighbours, and ultimately the law. They did things like keeping the curtains closed during the daytime, peeking out the windows and changing the license plates on their car every time they went out.

Their initial intention was to stay at this hide-out for a month or two. Near the end of two weeks, Clyde was getting nervous, and rightly so. The gang started to make plans to leave, but unfortunately, their date of departure was one day too late. If Clyde wanted to rest for a few weeks, he should have driven well out of their normal territory and rented a house that was isolated. In the now vacant apartment, the police found Buck's guitar, and prison release papers. They also found three long guns, which the gang in their haste left behind.

The five fugitives made their escape without too much damage to themselves. A shell grazed Blanche's arm. Buck had a bruise on his chest from a shell, and Clyde had a chest wound, which wasn't too serious. Jones was shot in the right side. The shell entered him from the front, grazed a rib, and went out the back. In the car, Blanche tried to help Jones, but there was blood all over. He was becoming weak and sleepy from the loss of blood.

The gang, after making their escape from Joplin, drove in a southerly direction on back roads. It started to rain, and before long, Clyde stopped to change a flat tire. He then started driving west, but the roads were muddy and wet, which hampered his speed.

Finally, the outlaws found a small country store, which had gas pumps. They filled the car with gas, checked the oil and bought some aspirin for Jones. The evening air was cold, and the rain kept falling. Clyde drove over several roads in a northwest direction, trying to find the main highway. About an hour after the sun went down, he came out to the highway and headed west through Oklahoma.

Chapter 5
Shamrock, Texas
April 14, 1933

By morning, the Barrow Gang reached Shamrock, Texas. After a long sleepless night of travelling, they decided to rent a cabin at a local tourist park. The cabin was small and dirty, but the gang made the best of it. Their priority was attending to their wounds and taking baths. After washing and drying herself, Blanche sat in one of the chairs in the room and started to cry. Her dream of having Buck go straight was shattered, and her life would now be changed forever.

After washing herself, Bonnie was the only one with clothes that looked respectable. However, with the gang's rapid departure from Joplin, they left their coats behind. Bonnie had no choice but to walk over to a small variety store next to the park in a summer dress. The morning air was cold, and she looked out of place, but they needed food and medical supplies.

Bonnie picked up some medical supplies and put them on the counter while the clerk was busy getting her food order. She tried to look innocent, but the scenes from the shootout the day before, were fresh in her memory. Bonnie paid for the order and returned to the cabin. The gang dressed their wounds and ate the food. At that point, some of them tried to sleep.

Just before noon, Blanche noticed a couple of cars driving in, and they parked outside the office. Two men got out of each vehicle, and she believed they were the law. Clyde and Buck were now awake and took a look. One of the men came out of the office and retrieved what looked like a file from one of the cars. He glanced towards the cabin, which the Barrows had rented, and went back into the office. Both Clyde and Buck decided it was time to go as they didn't want another shootout. The group quickly loaded the car and drove out a secondary exit furthest from the office. They made their escape, and drove the rest of that day, trying to stay on back roads as much as possible.

With the car's gas tank almost empty and short on money, the gang found a gas station in a quiet community. They relieved it of money, food, and gas. As darkness fell, Clyde stole a car. Cars were easy to steal, and Clyde felt safer in a freshly stolen car. The gang then robbed a larger store, this time getting away with clothes, food, medical supplies, and more money. The Barrow Gang drove through the night and finally pulled into a wooded area, where they slept. The gang always made sure one of them stayed awake on guard duty while the others slept.

Chapter 6
Wellington, a Test of Bonnie & Clyde's Love for Each Other.
June 10, 1933

By June 1933, the law was starting to make more of an effort to close in on Bonnie and Clyde. Clyde was continuously driving from state to state, trying to starve of capture. The cat and mouse game put a lot of pressure on Clyde, and it caught up with him on June 10, 1933, near Wellington, Texas.

Clyde liked to drive fast, and that day he was on his way to a rendezvous with Buck and Blanche. He was travelling down U.S. Hwy 83 and missed a detour sign. The sign had been erected; to alert motorists, the bridge across the Salt Fork of the Red River had been washed out. When he realized there was no bridge, it was too late. He could not stop the car in time, so he swerved and landed in the dried-up river bed and rolled to a stop.

Special Note

The following story is the most likely one about this innocent. As I mention before, there are so many versions of various B&C incidents that it has become impossible in many cases to know what the facts are. One would believe that on-site witnesses to an event would tell the facts, but we see witnesses giving different versions of what happened. The Wellington car accident also has several variations of the details, which occurred. However, minor details be them fact, or fiction does not take away from the accident and what took place. For example, when help arrived at the accident site, some accounts tell us, Clyde and Jones were trying to rescue Bonnie. Other accounts tell us Clyde and Jones were still in the car dazed, but unhurt. The problem here is when help arrived; if Clyde and Jones were still in the car dazed, the rescuers must have noticed all the guns that were lying around. Normal people don't travel with an arsenal of weapons. Therefore, they would surely have realized these three people were probably wanted criminals.

I believe Clyde was not travelling that fast at the time of the accident. The Cartwrights put the time at dusk around 10:00 pm. If that were true, it would have been nearly dark. A small wood barrier probably held the sign, stating the bridge was out. Its location was most likely close to the end of the road. It was more likely, Clyde did not see the sign until the last instant, and by that time, it would have been too late for him to stop safely. The Ford coupe ran through the barrier and tumbled down the embankment, rolling a couple of times before coming to rest on its side.

It was more reasonable to believe Clyde and Jones were probably shaken up a little but were able to get themselves out of the car. Bonnie was pinned inside the car. The battery on that car was probably under the floorboard in a compartment, which had a metal door resting in a grove on the floorboard. The rolling car caused the door to open and battery acid to spill out. Unfortunately, Bonnie was sitting on the same side as the battery and acid ran down her leg. The story goes on to say the car was scorched a bit, but that was not an issue for the story.

Clyde and Jones worked frantically to free Bonnie, as she was screaming in immeasurable pain. Battery acid, when in contact with human flesh, eats it away. Just the thought of how much pain she had to endure is mind-boggling. I would also think she was drifting in and out of consciousness. One account states, she was begging Clyde to shoot her dead, but if that is true, he could not do it.

The story continues by saying the accident happened just below a house, which was owned by the Pritchard family. The Pritchard's had visitors that evening. When the accident happened, three of the menfolk rushed down to the accident site to offer assistance. On arriving, they found Clyde and Jones trying to rescue a woman in a car who was hurt badly. Battery acid had dripped on her leg, and she was in pain. With the extra help, they were able to free the woman who was then carried up to the house.

Under those circumstances, Clyde and Jones would have made their intentions known right away. They would have picked up their weapons and taken control of the situation. Even so, there was a young woman in severe pain, and she needed immediate medical attention. These kind folks did what many would have done under the same circumstances, and that was to help the injured.

It is reasonable to believe, Clyde would have made an extra effort to convince these kind folks that nothing bad was going to happen to them. However, one of the men either slipped away unnoticed or persuaded Clyde to let him go for a doctor. Clyde was no fool; he knew Bonnie needed help. Regardless of how it happened, the story states Alonzo Cartwright went for the Doctor and, at the same time, notified the law about the accident.

There was one key piece of information that was unknown. Did Cartwright notify the police about all the guns, or did he keep quiet? Two officers were dispatched to check out the accident. They did not bring any special weapons or extra men. We, therefore, have to assume that Cartwright made no mention of the guns. To the police, it was just another car accident with injuries.

However, when the police arrived at the house, they were immediately taken as prisoners. Cartwright did not come back at the same time as the police, because as the story goes, he had car trouble. Anyway, Clyde shot out the tires on two old cars at the house then drove off in the police car, with Bonnie, Jones and the two hostages.

However, at some point during the incident, Jones shot Gladys Cartwright in the hand, as he believed she was going for a gun. Gladys was the young woman who cared for Bonnie.

Chapter 7
Fort Smith, Arkansas
June 15, 1933

When the Barrow Gang left Wellington, Clyde headed for Fort Smith, Arkansas. They arrived on June 15, 1933, and rented two cabins at the Twin Cities Tourist Camp in Fort Smith. On the trip to Arkansas, and after they arrived, Bonnie was in unbearable pain. Her only relief came when she would slip into an unconscious state. Clyde rarely left her side, and he was struggling with what he should do. Their affection, for one another, had blossomed into a love that was real, and some newspapers compared it to Romeo and Juliet. Romeo and Juliet was a play written by William Shakespeare, but Bonnie and Clyde were the real thing.

On June 18, Clyde drove to Dallas to pick up Bonnie's sister, Billie Jean. He figured if anyone could nurse Bonnie back to health, it would be her sister. When Clyde arrived back at Fort Smith, Bonnie was in a coma. The details are missing, but somehow either Clyde or Billie Jean got talking to the daughter of the owner of the tourist court. She was a nurse and came over to have a look at Bonnie's leg. She immediately knew Bonnie needed a doctor. Without proper care, Bonnie was in danger of dying.

The nurse contacted a doctor friend of hers, and the doctor started intensive treatment on Bonnie. The story says, neither the owner of the court, the nurse or the doctor knew who they were helping. However, I find that hard to believe. You have a young woman with a leg that has been eaten away by battery acid almost down to the bone. She should be in a hospital, yet these people who brought her to this place are saying no. I believe Clyde and Billie Jean, in a moment of desperation, put their trust in the hands of strangers to save the life of Bonnie. If they hadn't done that, Bonnie would certainly have died at that court.

Billie Jean, years later, made a statement that surely cements human values and says we are a nation of people who do care for one another. The following happened in a courtroom, when the nurse who helped Bonnie, refused under oath to reveal the identity of the woman (Billie Jean) who also helped Bonnie through that trying period. It goes to show that human kindness can move people to do great things.

Within less than a week, the gang was running low on money. Clyde now had to depend on his brother Buck and Jones to refill the empty coffers. On June 23, Buck and Jones robbed the R.L. Brown Grocery Market in Fayetteville. They were involved in a car accident while returning to the gang's hideout. The pair then had a shootout with two officers (who responded to the accident) on U.S. Hwy 71, north of Alma. The officers were Marshal Henry Humphrey (who died three days later in a hospital from a chest wound) and Deputy Sheriff Ansel Salyers.

At some point in Bonnie's recovery, she insisted that Clyde take Billie Jean back to Texas before she became involved with the law. Bonnie, under no circumstances, wanted her sister to become a fugitive.

With the heat on from Buck killing the lawman, the Barrow gang could not risk staying at Fort Smith. Soon they were on the move, driving the back roads on their way to Texas with Billie Jean in tow. They did this for about two weeks, camping out at night, and stopping to rub ointments on Bonnie's legs. Finally, they arrived in Sherman, Texas and put Billie Jean on a bus headed for Dallas.

Chapter 8
The Gunfight at Platte City, Missouri,
The Red Crown
July 20, 1933

Clyde's luck took a turn for the worst when the gang had to shoot their way out of the Joplin, Missouri hideout in mid-April 1933. With rolls of film left behind, the law shared the gang's pictures with papers across the country. With their faces known, the Barrow Gang was finding it hard to remain anonymous. The law was on their trail, and Clyde was starting to feel the pressure, which was causing him to make critical errors in judgment.

The car accident in which Bonnie was hurt and almost died was like a weight around his neck. However, Clyde was not the cold-blooded killer the law and papers branded him with. He was a young man in love with his true partner, Bonnie. A genuine killer would have abandoned his woman to save his skin, but not Clyde. Bonnie was his whole world, and to save her life, Clyde gambled, hoping the other members of his gang could come through.

Clyde's judgment became foggy, and it was apparent to the other gang members when he decided to rent rooms at the Red Crown Tourist Court in Platte City, Missouri. Bonnie needed rest and medical attention, and Clyde could not see the impending danger at this court. His brother Buck agreed in principle; they needed to find somewhere to rest for a few days. When Clyde decided the Red Crown was a good choice, his brother got into an argument with him. That led to the two of them not talking to each other.

Buck's side of the argument had merit. He was concerned about this place. One month earlier, the Kansas City Massacre happened at its Union Station. Several law enforcement officers were killed, and the place was still considered hot by gangsters. Buck made the argument that they would be the only guests and would stand out like a sore thumb. He was also concerned about the tavern and restaurant. They were a busy place, which could mean trouble and the police.

In the end, either Clyde could not think clearly or was willing to take a big gamble. There was no dispute about Bonnie, she needed rest, but Clyde picked the worst possible location. His decision would lead to the eventual death of Buck and the capture of Blanche.

Emmett Breen, a banker and developer, built the Red Crown in 1931. The establishment was located at the junction of US 71 and Route 59 (now I-435). The tavern had a restaurant and ballroom located inside it and two cabins connected by a two-bay garage out behind it. The Red Crown was located at a busy intersection. The question then arises, why did the developer choose to build only two cabins? As the case with much development in those years, it was probably due to a lack of money.

Clyde pulled into a filling station located across from the Red Crown. He noticed the two cabins that were behind the tavern and mentioned to his partners that it looked like a good place to stay. The filling station attendant told Clyde if he wanted to rent the cabins, he could inquire at the Red Crown office. The office was located in the tavern building.

Before driving over, Clyde pulled one of his tricks to disguise the size of his party, and that was covering Jones and Buck with blankets in the back seat. Of course, Blanche was the guinea pig, and she would be the one going over to rent the two cabins for a night. Unfortunately, Blanch was wearing tight, sexy riding breeches, which were something, locals in this city had never seen before. The get-up immediately caught the attention of manager Neal Houser who became suspicious. The truth is her choice of clothing was so unusual that the locals, who noticed her, began discussing it.

 Everyone except Clyde thought it was a risky plan to stay at this honky-tonk place. When Blanche made her flouncy entrance into the tavern office, things went downhill from there. The gang had no way of knowing this place was a favourite gathering spot for the Missouri Highway Patrol. During this era, police cars did not have two-way radios in them. This spot was a convenient place for officers and their supervisors to meet at lunchtime and exchange information.

Blanche rented the two cabins for the night. She paid with a handful of small change. The manager then watched out the tavern's rear window as Clyde backed the car into the garage, which was considered gangster style. Shortly after, Blanche went over to the Tavern's restaurant and ordered five take out dinners and five beers. She paid with a handful of small change. Of course, she was wearing tight-fitting trousers, which caused everyone to stare at her again. The manager insisted on following Blanche back to the cabin so that he could record the car's license plate number. Clyde refused to let him into the garage. Everything about these people made Houser even more suspicious.

By the next day, the staff at the Red Crown had noticed the visitors were peeking out the windows. They refused to allow any of the staff into the cabins for cleaning and were staying hidden inside except for Blanche.

At lunchtime, Blanche strolled over to the restaurant in her get-up, ordered five meals and paid with small change. While Blanche was waiting for the food, she had a feeling someone was not only staring at her but was sizing her up. Her instincts were correct. Platte County Sheriff Holt Coffey was paying very close attention to her. Clyde had told her to pay the rent on the rooms for another night, but Blanche had a bad feeling about the situation. She returned to the cabins, without paying for another night to talk to Clyde about the situation. Clyde, safely nestled inside the cabin, ignored her observations, another mistake on his part.

Houser had originally spoken about his suspicions to Captain William Baxter of the Missouri Highway Patrol. The Captain then started wondering, who was in those cabins with Oklahoma plates on their car.

Later that day, Sheriff Coffey got a call from Louis Bernstein, the druggist at Platte City Drugs. He told Coffey about a young, attractive woman, who came into the drug store wearing skin-tight pants and knee-high boots. She purchased medical supplies that were often used for skin burns. Both the drug store and law enforcement agencies had been alerted by Oklahoma, Texas and Arkansas officials to be on the watch for strangers needing certain medical supplies.

Baxter and Coffey were now convinced they had members of the dangerous Barrow Gang inside the cabins. They knew all too well about the arsenal of weapons Clyde Barrow carried. Coffey knew the gang's members would not hesitate to bring their full firepower to bear against anyone who dared to challenge them. He also knew Clyde was an experienced driver and gunman from reading about his previous shoot-outs. The lawmen knew it would be suicide on their part to try to take this gang without more help and better equipment.

Coffey headed over to nearby Kansas City. The police department was much larger and had bullet-proof shields, armoured cars, tear gas launchers and machine guns. Coffey explained his suspicions to Sheriff Tom Bash. The sheriff balked at the idea of sending men and equipment over to what was probably nothing. He refused Coffey's request. However, Coffey was determined, and eventually, Bash agreed to send some men and equipment over.

Coffey and Baxter figured they now stood a chance of being on an even playing field with the gang. However, they would soon find out their light machine guns, bullet-proof vests, and the armoured car was no match for the BAR Automatic Rifles that fired metal piercing shells. These BAR rifles could cut down men and equipment as easy as a hot knife going through butter.

Word soon got around town; there could be another Kansas City Massacre at the Red Crown. Coffey decided to wait till closing and give the public a chance to leave the area, before attempting a take-down. The tension and sense of action was building in everyone except the Barrow Gang, who thought it was going to be a quiet night.

As darkness fell, Blanche came out of her cabin and walked over to the Tavern to get soap and fresh towels, oblivious to what was soon to take place. As she walked into the place, everyone stopped talking, and as she left, the talking resumed. When she returned to the cabin, she told Clyde about the situation, but again Clyde acted as if it was nothing. A short time later, Jones emerged from the cabin and went across the road to Slim's Castle to order food.

By 1:00 am, most of the regulars at the Red Crown had left. The lawmen who were about to engage the Barrow gang had done everything they could do to make themselves ready. The campaign tonight would be a coordinated effort by well prepared and armed officers. The team of officers was thirteen an unlucky number, but the raid was going ahead. At least the lawmen involved knew exactly what they were up against.

Like always eyewitnesses and lawmen involved, have told several different versions of how the gun battle played out. There was a gun battle, and it most likely went something as described below:

The officers pulled four of their patrol cars into a defensive position to give themselves cover. One office pulled the armoured car up to the garage doors to block the gangster's car inside. From that point, Coffey stood up with a boilerplate shield. He used a megaphone aimed at the cabins to voice the message, "This is the law, come out with your hands high in the air."

The law didn't have to wait long for a response. Within thirty seconds, all hell broke loose, as armour-piercing shells started hitting the patrol cars. The officers ducked down, as the sound of the shells ripping through the car's metal scared the hell out of them. Then Buck and Jones started firing their BARs automatic rifles, and the stream of shells turned into a hailstorm. Coffey was lucky, as some shells hit his shield and pushed him backwards, like being hit by a high-pressure water hose, but the boilerplate did its job. Coffey was unhurt.

The officers managed to return some fire with their substandard 45-calibre Thompson machine guns, but they were no match for the BARs. Later they found several shells from the BARs were lodged in the kitchen walls of the Tavern. Shells were found not only in the Red Crown but in private cars, and some made it across the road to Slim's Castle. The thundering sound of the BAR's fire woke people for miles around in the quiet night air.

Clyde and Jones went through the inside door from their cabin to the garage, where their car was parked. Clyde peeked out the garage door and noticed the armoured police vehicle parked in front of the doors. The police vehicle had only light armour in a couple of places, and Clyde discovered it was not bulletproof. Clyde opened fire on it, and the BAR's shells penetrated the metal with no problem. The officer sitting at the wheel was hit in both knees. Clyde did a lot of damage to the car. One rifle shell struck the horn button, and it started to blare.

The lawmen, for some reason, assumed this was a stop fire signal, and they did. A handful of officers went as far as backing away from the cabin. Clyde pumped more shells into the armoured car, and the driver decided he had enough. With both knees shattered, he managed to back the car away from the garage doors and out of range of the guns. Then the story goes that an officer behind the cabin fired a tear-gas shell, which overshot the cabin and landed on the roadway. The wind carried the thick eye-burning gas back over the officers. The lawmen then believing the gangsters had tear-gas and who knows what else, started running for cover as they were expecting a new wave of BAR fire.

Clyde saw what was taking place and could not believe his luck. The car blocking his escape was gone, and most of the lawmen had not only stopped firing but were caught up in tear gas. While all this was happening, Jones was spraying the entire front area where the other police cars were parked with fire. Clyde then ordered Jones to help Bonnie get in the car as he took over-spraying the confused posse with shells.

If Buck and Blanche had a door into the garage, the entire outlaw gang might have escaped with no injuries. No such door existed, and when Buck and his wife made a run for it, a couple of the officers who saw them opened up with their Tommy guns. One bullet caught Buck in the left temple and exited out his forehead. Clyde saw his brother go down and shouted at Jones to provide some cover fire. Clyde rushed outside, and with the help of Blanche, they got Buck inside the garage and dumped him in the car. All this happened within the time span of about 45 seconds.

With everyone in the car, Clyde stepped on the gas and fired his automatic shotgun out the driver's side window as he sped away. Jones was firing his automatic rifle out the passenger side window. All the posse could do was duct as the car roared past them. One officer managed to fire one more round from his machine gun as the gang escaped. A couple of shells shattered the rear window on the car, sending glass into Blanche's eyes. The gangsters and their car vanished into the night.

One lawman tried to convince some others to take up the pursuit, but the posse members had enough. They realized the Barrows, if this is who they were, had superior firepower.

As the night breeze cleared the smoked from the air, the lawmen assessed the situation. The outlaws had fired hundreds of rounds of armour-piercing shells. This was far more than any other gunfight the Barrows had been in. Despite the night air being filled with shells, the posse members-only sustained minor injuries. Five of the lawmen had flesh wounds. Three onlookers, who thought they were far enough away, had flesh wounds. Four police cars and the armoured car were pounded by fire. Two private vehicles had a dozen or more bullet holes in them, and the Red Crown building had many shells embedded in the outside and inside walls.

The posse knew they had hit one of the members, but could only guess at how severe his injuries were. However, for Clyde, one of his closest allies, his brother would die from his head wound.

Inside the cabin occupied by Clyde, the lawmen found the uneaten sandwiches and more weapons, which the gang had to leave behind. The next day, large crowds of sightseers came out to look at the aftermath and hopefully recover souvenirs. The two cabins suffered damage as there were bullet holes everywhere.

After, Leaving the Red Crown
July 21, 1933

As the Barrow Gang escaped into the darkness of the night from the Red Crown, there was no celebration of another successful shootout. Yes, they managed to get away, but the price they paid was heavy.

Clyde's Ford V8 sedan was shot up. The lawmen had successfully shot his rear tires and shattered the car's rear window. In the backseat, Blanche was screaming because the glass was in both her eyes. She was cradling Buck's head in her lap as he babbled incoherently. He had been shot in the head and was down for the count, and Bonnie's leg was bleeding again.

Figuring the lawmen would give chase and block nearby roads, Clyde went to plan "B." He headed north on US Hwy-71 and managed to get the car to Farmers Lane and Winan Road. At that point, he told Jones to steal a car jack from a nearby house. While waiting for Jones to return, Clyde attended to Buck's head wound and Bonnie's leg, which was bleeding.

On Jones returning with a jack, Clyde changed tires and threw the flat one in the ditch with some bloody rags. Clyde continued driving the back roads fearing the law had set up roadblocks on the main highways. He finally found a country filling station, where he filled up, and then headed north for Iowa. That's one version of the getaway. Regardless of how they accomplished it, they did getaway.

The Barrow gang pulled into Caledonia, Iowa, early Thursday morning, July 20, 1933. They licked their wounds and tried to get some rest. Later that morning, the group broke camp and headed for Dexfield, Iowa.

In the late afternoon, the Barrows abandoned camp at Caledonia, was found. It was confirmed, the campsite was the Barrows because a newspaper called, "The Country Gentleman" was one of the items found. That newspaper belonged to a Mr. White. It was lifted from his rural mailbox at Yale, Iowa, on Tuesday afternoon, July 18, 1933. Other items found at the campsite were bloody half-burnt clothing.

Chapter 9
The Gunfight at Dexfield Park

The gang pulled into a 20-acre nature reserve close to Dexfield called Dexfield Park, late in the evening on July 20, 1933. They made a campsite on a wooded hilltop overlooking the park site. The gang stayed there for the next four days. (July 21, 22, 23 and 24)

By early morning on July 21, 1933, the gang was suffering. Buck was delirious, suffering from a savage head wound and near death. Blanche was nursing her eyes as she would never see again from one of them. The healing scabs on Bonnie's leg were bleeding. All their medical supplies were left behind at the Red Crown, where they had made a hasty escape the day before. For the first time in his life, Clyde was weary, scared and wanted this nightmare to end.

Clyde and Jones, the two with the least amount of injuries, headed down to a nearby river. It was early morning, and they washed the blood off themselves and cleaned their clothes. They then returned to the campsite with water to wash Bonnie, Buck and Blanche.

The gang now found themselves in desperate need of medical supplies. With a shot up car, Clyde was also in need of a new one. Desperate situations call for desperate measures. Clyde gambled that his ailing friends would be safe for a short while. Clyde and Jones left the others at the campsite and took a drive over to Perry, Iowa. Clyde selected a 1932 Model A Ford belonging to Ed Stoner and borrowed it permanently.

When Clyde and Jones returned to the campsite, Clyde dropped off Jones. He then drove into Dexter alone, where he purchased supplies. Clyde bought some shirts, trousers and socks with the help of a clerk at one clothing store. The clerk's name was John Love, and he had a second job acting as Dexter's night police officer. Halfway through the sale, Clyde noticed the clerk had a law badge pinned to his shirt pocket when he dropped a shirt on the floor and bent over to pick it up. His sweater parted enough to give Clyde the view. Clyde kept his cool, completed the transaction and walked out of the store very casually.

Clyde returned to his latest stolen car and put the clothing in the car. He then went into a local restaurant and ordered five dinners to go. He paid for them, and the waitress told him it would be a few minutes before they were ready. Clyde told her he would be back shortly as he had another errand to run. Later, the waitress told local authorities he was cute and extremely polite.

From the restaurant, Clyde walked into the local pharmacy and purchased medical supplies. His purchase did not alarm anyone, as times were lean, and many people treated their injuries, even serious ones, as they could not afford to go to a doctor. Clyde then picked up his takeout food, bought some gas and headed back to the campsite.

One local citizen who was in the restaurant at the time of Clyde's visit, later indicated, he though Clyde looked familiar. That could be true. Clyde made a point of not ripping off certain towns in his circle of travels through the mid-south. He referred to these towns as safe-haven pit stops, wherein an emergency, he could purchase goods and feel safe. According to the townspeople of Dexter, Clyde made several trips into town to buy food.

While Clyde was gone to Dexter, Jones talked on a personal level with Buck, who was awake. Jones admitted he was scared of Clyde. He believed Clyde was just using him. When the time came, he believed Clyde would throw him to the dogs like an old soup bone. According to Jones's confession later, Buck encouraged him to break ranks with Clyde.

A group of twelve Girl Scouts led by Della Growley was out hiking in the Dexfield Park early Saturday morning, July 22. They accidentally walked right into the Barrow campsite. Later, one of the scouts indicated the Barrows acted surprised. The girl scouts said, "Good morning to the gang," not realizing who they were, and the pleasantry was returned. The next day, one of the girl scouts came face to face with Bonnie and Clyde in Dexter. The girl said, "good morning." Bonnie and Clyde looked at her with a puzzled look until she said, "I was one of the scouts yesterday morning, who walked into your campsite in Dexfield Park." The girl then said," The two smiled at her, and Bonnie wished her a nice day." The girl thought to herself, they make a nice couple and went on her way.

Sunday afternoon Henry Nve was out for a walk and picking wild fruit when he noticed two cars parked in a remote section of the park. He kept himself hidden as he made his way closer. To him, it looked like one of the cars had bullet holes. Then he noticed one of the women had a patch over one eye, and a man's head was bandaged. The whole affair looked suspicious, so Nve contacted John Love, a local Marshall.

The two men then returned to the park with binoculars. John could clearly see the car was shot up. Love then contacted Dallas County Sheriff Clint Knee in Adel. The Sheriff heard reports the Barrow gang had been reported in the area. Love, not knowing for sure if this was the Barrow Gang, told Knee to bring his heavy artillery to Dexter.

By Sunday afternoon, Clyde knew his brother Buck was not going to make it. He decided, as soon as the group felt a little better, they would leave for Texas to bring his injured brother home.

Love and Knee determined, this was, in fact, the Barrow Gang, and they started to make plans for a Monday Morning July 24, raid. The posse included DesMoines police officers as well as a dentist named Dr. Kellar. Mr. Kellar owned a machine gun. The posse knew they would have to try to hem the gang in, so they called on local citizens who had shotguns and rifles.

The group converged on the site at 6:00 am on July 24 and quickly took up positions. They blocked the road leading into the park along with a bridge. The police approached the campsite from the west. The Barrow Gang was up and eating their breakfast when they noticed movements in the brush around their camp. The posse without fair warning opened fire, in what would become the biggest gunfight in Ballas Country history.

The gang still had Browning Automatic Rifles (BARs) and returned fire with them. The posse believing they had the upper hand, immediately retreated under deadly heavy fire. This move gave the gang time to reposition themselves in an attempt to escape.

The Barrows piled into the closest car, which was the shot-up one, and Clyde gunned the car. It shot forward, and with a little luck, they may have broken through the police line. However, Clyde took a slug in the arm and lost control of the car, which ran over a tree stump. Unable to free the vehicle, the gang headed for their second car, but the posse opened fire on it, making it useless as a getaway car. Their only choice was to run. Buck was hit in the back and flopped to the ground. Blanche refused to leave him. Bonnie took some pellets to her midsection, and Jones was hit in the head by a glancing shot.

Clyde took up a defensive position and told Jones to help Bonnie to the Raccoon River and get her across. Clyde began to fire at the advancing posse, and this gave Jones and Bonnie time to escape. Clyde started to fall back and soon reached the river. He crossed it and met up with his two friends. The three desperadoes continued to fall back and made their way behind Spillers Cemetery. All three were wounded and losing blood.

Clyde, by himself, approached the farmhouse of Vallie Feller. Mr. Feller's son Marvelle and a hired man were attending to the morning chores when they saw a small blooded man emerge from the cornfield. The man was Clyde, and he pointed a handgun at the two and told them he needed help. Clyde whistled, and Jones carried Bonnie up to the fence. The two men then helped Bonnie across the fence. Clyde told them to put Bonnie in the backseat of their family car, which was a 1929 Plymouth. With Bonnie in the car, Clyde and Jones got in and took off. It is interesting to note after Jones was captured in Texas, he later confessed to the fact that Clyde's handgun was empty.

Clyde drove the Feller car to Polk City, which was about 38 miles to the northeast of Dexter. Somehow they wrecked the car, so they held up a filling station and stole a Ford V8. For the next few days, little is known about where the gang headed and what they did. However, on July 28, the stolen Ford was found on a side road close to Broken Bow, Nebraska. Inside the car were bloody bandages and medicine bottles. There was no sign of the gang as once again, Clyde made a successfully escaped.

The gang then doubled back to Guthrie Center. It was reported, the gang escaped again from a posse in Guthrie, mostly due to the expert driving of Clyde. Clyde was last seen about 75 miles north of Sioux City.

Meanwhile, back at Dexter Park, most of the posse had gathered around Buck and Blanche, who were now their prisoners. One of the lawmen grabbed Blanche and pulled her away from Buck. He was dying and helpless. Buck had a hole in his skull and was taken to a nearby hospital. Blanche never saw Buck again and was not allowed to attend his funeral.

As for Blanche, the police returned her to Platte City. She was charged with assault with intent to kill and held on a fifteen thousand dollar bond.

Jones stayed with Bonnie and Clyde until they were well enough to survive on their own. After leaving the gang, Jones got work in a Texas cotton field but was arrested by authorities not long after. Eventually, he was turned over to Dallas Deputy Sheriff Ted Hinton. Hinton was a man who shared a history with the gang and would play a role in their ultimate demise.

The Aftermath of Dexfield

Buck and Blanche were taken to a small hospital clinic in Dexter from the shootout in Dexfield Park. Buck told the doctor, the only treatment he received for his head wound was aspirin, and his friends poured hydrogen peroxide into the wound. Meanwhile, Blanche was taken into a separate room to have her eyes examined. A police officer then transported Buck to a hospital in Perry, where a bullet was removed from his chest. There was little else doctors could do, and a few days later, Buck died.

News of Buck and Blanche's capture reached Dallas the same day as the shootout. In a show of human compassion, Dallas County Sheriff Smoot Schmid gave Buck's mother Cumie a letter of introduction. This letter would be her introduction to the law authorities in Perry. Schmid made the plea that Cumie be allowed to see her dying son. In a further show of compassion, Schmid's office paid for the travel expenses to Perry and back.

Cumie did arrive in Perry and was allowed to visit, but Buck had taken a turn for the worst and did not recognize her. Buck finally fell into a coma, and passed away in his mother's arms, on July 29. Even the law authorities in Perry showed the mother compassion in her hour of grief. The body of Buck Barrow was transported back to Dallas, where the family buried him in the Western Heights Cemetery.

Buck's mother wept through the service, while his father, Henry, kept his head bowed. The Sheriff's office sent several deputies to guard the chapel in case Clyde tried to attend. After the service ended, there was a rumour that Clyde was there in disguise. As for Blanche, she was not allowed to attend Buck's funeral.

Chapter 10
On the Trail of Bonnie and Clyde

It was now the beginning of August 1933, and for Bonnie and Clyde, their glory days were coming to an end. However, as in life, their legend would grow in death.

With the loss of his brother Buck, Jones, ready to call it quits and Bonnie a cripple, Clyde was feeling the strain of being on the run. He confided in Bonnie and told her he had one more serious mission to complete before calling it quits. That mission was a raid on Eastham Prison in Texas. Bonnie begged him to forget about that. She tried to persuade him to move on now before the law killed him. The anger and memories were burnt deep in Clyde, and he was obsessed with his mission.

Until his death in May 1934, Clyde continued to steal cars and commit robberies. The two most notable came in August 1933, when Clyde and Jones robbed a National Guard Armory in Plattville, Illinois. They made off with more guns and ammo. The second came on January 16, 1934, when Bonnie and Clyde raided the Eastham Prison, setting convicts free. The convicts were Ray Hamilton, Henry Methvin, Hilton Bybee, John French and Joe Palmer.

After the successful hold-up of the armoury in late August 1933, Jones told Bonnie and Clyde, he wanted out. He told them he wanted to go back to his mother's home. To Jones's surprise, Clyde understood and even coached him on what to tell authorities if he was ever caught. Clyde told him to tell the law that he was forced by the gang to stay and commit robberies.

As September 1933 set in, Bonnie, Clyde and Jones set out for Dallas. It was now five months since they had seen their families, and a lot had happened. The trio arrived in Dallas and immediately dropped Jones off. Jones left for Houston to be with his mother, and Bonnie and Clyde contacted their families.

Although Bonnie and Clyde had a few weeks to lick their wounds, the couple looked like they had just come off a battlefield. Clyde had scars, scratches, and his once youthful face was showing the strain of premature middle age. Bonnie was a cripple, getting around with the help of crutches. She was no longer the cute, attractive woman she once was.

September 8, 1933, was the reunion date. The spot was a deserted location just outside of Dallas. Both mothers were stunned at the couple's appearance, especially Bonnie, who looked more like a skeleton than a young woman.

Clyde then started telling the two families about their hardships, since the shootout at Dexfield. There was no safe place to stay at night, so they slept in the car, usually parked in remote country fields. The law was always close behind them.

Cumie explained to Clyde, why Buck did not have a headstone on his grave yet. She told Clyde, the end is coming for you, and we can only afford one stone. She told Clyde, we are going to bury you with your brother, and buy the tombstone then. Clyde agreed with his mother, even offering a saying for the stone.

In October 1933, Billie Jean's two children died of a serious illness. Bonnie adored the two kids, and when they died, she fell into a depression. Emma tried desperately to get Bonnie to leave Clyde before it was too late. Billie Jean agreed with Emma and tried herself, sister to sister, to get Bonnie away from Clyde. It was all in vain as Bonnie told everyone, she would stay with Clyde until the end and die with him.

While Clyde stayed close to Dallas, the law was aware of their presence and tried twice to ambush them, but came up empty. Clyde was a slippery character and had more lives than a house cat.

In mid-January 1934, the Barrow Gang raided Eastham Prison and set several prisoners free. This was the last straw for Texas Prison officials. Bonnie and Clyde made them look like fools, and the hunt was now on.

Frank Hamer, the man who would eventually lead a posse to ambush Bonnie and Clyde was born on March 17, 1884, in Fairview, Texas. His birth name was Francis Augustus Hamer. It is interesting to note that in the Movie, Lonesome Dove; it is rumoured that is how they chose the first name for the Texas Ranger character, Augustus (Gus) McCrae. When Hamer became a teenager, it was the dying days of the old American West. They say the time period you grow up in and place set the values you will carry for the rest of your life. This was true for Frank Hamer. He would read stories about outlaws like Jesse James, law officials like the Texas Rangers and Gray areas of the law, enforced by bounty hunters.

As Hamer entered his late teens, he was a big man at 215 pounds and 6 feet 4 tall. He liked to scrap and had no trouble holding his own. It was reported in the early days before he joined the Texas Ranger, he had some bloody fights. However, he finally chose the right side of the law and joined the Texas Rangers in 1906.

Hamer became famous as a ranger in his time. However, his relationship with the rangers was a stormy one. Several times he quit rangering for various reasons, but would always return to them.

In early 1934, when Bonnie and Clyde raided Eastham Prison and freed several convicts, it was the last straw for Lee Simmons. He was the top dog at the facility. Simmons called for Hamer to track them down and kill them. He made it clear to Hamer; he didn't care how it was done. Hamer dodged the job at first, claiming the money was no-good. Simmons assured him he would be allowed first dibs on whatever they recovered from the Barrow Gang. In those days, collectors were starting to pay some hefty prices for original guns. At that time, Hamer was not a ranger any longer but agreed to take the job as a civilian.

That set the stage for the most famous manhunt of all times. Hamer never made it public, but secretly, this was going to be the crown jewel in his bounty hunting career. It was reported he had already killed 51 men as a law officer, but hunting down Bonnie and Clyde was trophy material.

By January 1934, Clyde had recruited new men and had them trained. He was now back in the swing of robbing stores, banks and anything else, which looked easy. During this time, he was still close to Dallas, but out of concern for his own life and that of Bonnies, he would leave her with one of the families. Because of Bonnie's serious leg injury, she couldn't even drive a car.

While Clyde continued his life as a criminal, Hamer had built himself a wooden wall in his makeshift office. Hamer hung a large map of the southern United States on the wall. He began filling up the map with colored markers and dates showing Bonnie and Clyde's travels and their robberies. It was a slow, time-consuming job, but in the end, Hamer was catching up to Clyde. In fact, near the end, Hamer could predict with reasonable accuracy, where Bonnie and Clyde were likely to hit next.

One of the convicts Clyde set free from Eastham was a man named Henry Methvin. He was not a huge man, but bigger than Clyde. Clyde took a liking to this recruit probably because, the guy followed instructions and did not question Clyde's orders.

Now here is something worth mentioning. Clyde liked to think of himself as a modern-day Jesse James. Bonnie was interested in outlaws of the old west before she met Clyde. She was probably the one who told Clyde the story about Jesse, thus raising his interest. Anyway, the James Gang was shot up badly in the bungled Northfield, Minnesota bank job. They were trying to rob the First National Bank on September 7, 1876. Frank and Jesse James managed to escape, but the rest of their gang was killed except for one man.

You can compare this directly to Bonnie and Clyde at Dexfield Park. Although they were not trying to rob a bank, they were trying to rest, while tending to their wounds. The surprise attack further depleted their gang and left them with more wounds.

Jesse James was forced to hire new outlaws, and one of them was a man named Bob Ford. This recruit would eventually shoot Jesse in the back for a pardon. It happened much the same way to Clyde. He hired Methvin, and then the kid's old man betrayed Bonnie and Clyde, to the Hamer posse for a pardon.

As the winter days passed, Hamer was slowly getting closer to Clyde's way of thinking. The one thing Hamer never tried to do, was go directly into

Clyde's home territory of West Dallas. If Clyde suspected that Hamer was on his trail, it would probably spoil the progress he had made, in figuring out Clyde's movements. Instead, Hamer was collecting all the information he could and working on a plan to trap Clyde somewhere.

In the meantime, Clyde was continuing to rob banks, but tensions were running high with one of his recruits. Ray Hamilton decided he would only stay with the gang if Clyde let him bring his girlfriend, Mary, along on jobs. By this time, Bonnie was with Clyde again, but all she could do was sit in the car while the men robbed banks. Raymond's new girl Mary was nothing but trouble, as far as Bonnie was concerned.

Clyde caught Raymond stealing money from the gang. A short time later, Bonnie overheard Raymond and Mary, making plans to knock Clyde off. They were going to take over the gang themselves. Bonnie told Clyde what she heard, and that was it. Clyde came close to shooting Raymond, but in the end, told him to hit the road.

With Raymond's departure, the Barrow gang was down to three members Bonnie, Clyde and Henry Methvin. Clyde liked Henry because he did not question orders. Clyde now made an extra effort to keep Henry satisfied. One sure thing Henry liked was travelling to Louisiana to see his parents and relatives. Clyde figured this was a small price to pay to have a loyal partner.

It was now March 1934, and Hamer was travelling by himself in a car, trying to mimic Clyde's habits. Hamer was camping out and sleeping in his car some of the time. He would visit close by towns and travel the back roads. Lee Simmons had made no formal public announcement that he had hired Hamer to get Bonnie and Clyde. This gave Hamer the advantage, and he was hoping to catch them within a few weeks.

Chapter 11
Bonnie and Clyde Continue to Wreak Havoc

As reports came in about robberies, and sighting of the Barrow Gang, Hamer quickly noticed, Clyde was deviating off his normal routine. This would be a major setback if he continued these movements. However, around the middle of March 1934, Hamer was contacted by a sheriff Jordan from Bienville Parish in northwest Louisiana. The sheriff told Hanmer, someone had contacted him about setting a trap for Bonnie and Clyde. This man wanted his son to get a pardon for his crimes. The contact was Ivy Methvin, who was Henry Methvin's father. This could be the break Hamer was hoping for, and he left for Louisiana.

The story goes that Henry's parents were obsessed with getting Henry out of prison. Henry's father, Ivy, committed some robberies and got enough money to hire a lawyer. The story continues that it looked like they were going to be able to get their son out of prison. However, Bonnie and Clyde raided Eastham prison, and one of the convicts they set loose was Henry Methvin. Everyone knew about Bonnie and Clyde, and Ivy Methvin was reported to have said, "I'll shoot Clyde myself if I ever run into him."

Clyde took Henry Methvin under his wing, and they made a few trips to Louisiana so that Henry could visit his parents. Bonnie and Clyde like the area because it was an easy five-hour drive from Dallas on good roads. There were restaurants, filling stations and dry cleaners in the area. Clyde also liked the fact; the territory contained many remote wooded areas, where he and Bonnie could camp out.

However, all was not as it appeared to Clyde. Henry's father did not like Clyde and was scared of him. He hated Clyde for recruiting his son and was willing to make a deal with the law. This deal would allow the law to ambush Bonnie and Clyde in return for his son's freedom. Sheriff Jordan met with Ivy Methvin, about setting a trap for Bonnie and Clyde, but Jordan did not have the final say about a pardon. He told Methvin he would work it out with the law officials in Texas.

Bonnie and Clyde had planned to visit with their families for Easter of 1934. As usual, the meeting was to take place outside Dallas. This time, Clyde had chosen a remote road called Dover Road, which was a few miles outside Dallas on Highway 114. Everyone would meet there on Easter Sunday in the afternoon. The next thing to happen was just a case of bad luck for Bonnie and Clyde. The event would temporarily alter public sediment away from them, and would only enrage law officials. On Easter Sunday, Clyde parked his latest stolen Ford V8 about 400 feet down Dover Road.

Once again, there are several different versions of what took place. This has tainted the real truth, and it is now impossible to know how the event played out. This is more or less what happened. Three motorcycle officers were riding towards Dallas on Hwy 114. Apparently, one of them was riding well out in front, and the other two were further back. The lead officer went by Dover Road and kept going. However, one of the officers riding together, noticed Clyde's car. It was parked a distance down Dover Road. He motioned for the other officer riding with him, to follow him down the dirt road. The officer was going to check out the car. Henry noticed the two motorcycle cops coming down the road and told Clyde.

Clyde was going to kidnap the two officers and take them on a joyride before releasing them. He conveyed this message to Henry, but somehow Henry thought he meant, kill them. Henry had been drinking whisky, so his brain was probably, "out to lunch." Anyway, as the two cops pulled up in front of the Barrow car, Henry jumped up and fired his BAR rifle at one officer, hitting him in the chest. The officer fell to the ground, dead. Clyde started yelling at Henry, something to the effect are you crazy. The second officer, who was a rookie and working his first day, reached into his pocket for a shell to load into his shotgun. Clyde shot the officer, but only winged him so that he could be disarmed. Henry walked over to the downed officer, who was slightly wounded and pumped more lead into his chest, killing him.

According to Bonnie's diary, Clyde took a fit and started cursing at Henry. Clyde lifted his gun and threatened to shoot Henry, and leave him for the police. The three finally got into the car and got out of there. They drove out to Hwy 114, and headed away from Dallas, just as fast as the Ford could move. As they were driving away from the scene, Clyde was furious at Henry and was swearing at him.

A witness to the murder was a man named William Schieffer. He was sitting at the side of his house, located about 800 feet from the Barrow car. In his statement, he said, the person who approached the wounded officer was a woman. He said the woman aimed her gun at the officer, and pumped shells into his body. However, there were two other witnesses to the murder. An elderly couple had pulled to the side of the road at the corner of Hwy 114 and Dover Road. They had gotten out of their car and heard the first shot, which killed the officer. They then saw the smaller man, who would have been Clyde, shoot the second officer. They reported the officer was not badly wounded as he got to his knees. They then said, the larger man walked over to the officer and kicked him in the stomach, which caused him to fall to the ground. The bigger man opened fire on the officer. As this took place, the couple was about 400 feet from the shooting site.

The newspapers had both eyewitness accounts. They chose the one where the women shot the officer because they could say it was Bonnie and Clyde. The whole incident just sounded better with a woman doing the shooting. Unfortunately, the officer was engaged to be married in a few weeks. This cold-blooded killing caused public sediment to swing away from Bonnie and Clyde. To make matters even worse, the papers wrote that the police picked up cigar butts at the crime scene. The papers had already branded Bonnie as a "cigar-smoking gun moll," and this reinforced their claim. It was not a good day for the crime duo. The police called the two killings just outside of Texas, "The Grapevine Murders."

Hamer studied carefully how the Grapevine Murders went down. It was clear these two murders did not follow the set pattern of the Barrow Gang. If indeed it was the work of Clyde Barrow, something went wrong. He was a killer, but at the same time, he did not kill, unless he felt threatened. Hamer concluded it was probably the Barrow Gang. The two officers must have surprised the gang or else, Clyde had some inexperienced person with him, who jumped the gun. Hamer also concluded since Clyde was parked outside of Dallas on a dirt road off the main highway on Easter, he was probably there for a family gathering.

Every time Clyde killed or robbed banks Hamer's trophy kept getting bigger. Hamer also realized he needed to show Simmons he was making progress in his pursuit of the Barrow Gang. The senseless killing of the two officers near Grapevine brought a public outcry. The superintendent of the Texas Highway Patrol immediately offered a $1,000 reward for the Grapevine killers. Texas Governor Ferguson sweetened the pot by another five hundred dollars for each killer.

Clyde had a price on his head for past killings. Now, Bonnie had a price on her head, and she was innocent. Hamer was feeling the pressure. His methodical approach, of slowly sneaking up on the Barrows, and catching them by surprise, would not be good enough. Some of the state officials supporting him, as the person for the job were becoming restless.

Hamer needed to step it up a notch and show that he was actively hunting Bonnie and Clyde. Hamer needed a posse like in the old days of the west. The first man Hamer requested was B.M. (Maney), Gault. He was working for the Texas Highway Patrol, and they gladly reassigned him. Hamer then brought Bob Alcorn and Ted Hinton on board. The last two men had one big advantage; they knew Bonnie and Clyde and had seen them in person.

Hamer liked to work alone, but the prospects of trying to take on the Barrow Gang by himself scared him. If he got into a shootout with the gang and was killed, it would tarnish his reputation. The worst scenario would be, having Clyde take him, prisoner. If that ever happened, he would become the laughing stock of the Texas Rangers. The whole country would be laughing at him. Once Hamer got working with the posse members, he felt more comfortable. He still believed he could work with this posse, and have his trophy.

Hamer and his posse left Texas on April 4, 1934, and headed for Oklahoma. Clyde had a pattern of heading for this state, every time he committed major crimes in Texas. Various states, at that time, were a haven for criminals, because lawmen could not cross state lines legally, to chase their prey. This posse by unusual arrangement would be able to take down Bonnie and Clyde, wherever they cornered them. This was possible due to special regulations worked out by each state.

In Oklahoma, the posse stopped at various filling stations but came up empty. Then the posse got lucky when an attendant at one service station told them a woman and two men had stopped at the station. He said, "They were driving a new Ford V8." He also told them one of the men helped the woman, who had a bad limp to the public washroom. That was the one thing he remembered well.

The Barrow gang headed into the northeast corner of Oklahoma and stopped for the night on the shoulder of a state highway. Clyde would have found something more secluded, but the area had received so much rain the side roads were extremely muddy. The Barrows stopped close to the town of Commerce. Clyde parked the car for the night, between the towers of Lost Trail and the Crab Apple mines.

Unfortunately, the following morning was not going to be a good day for the law of Commerce. They received a report that a Ford was parked on the shoulder of the road, with some people sleeping inside. The police chief Percy Boyd, immediately assumed it was miners who probably had too much to drink the night before. This was not unusual for the area. The chief headed out in the morning with his constable Cal Campbell to check it out. The two men had no way of knowing they were going to come face to face with Clyde Barrow.

The sun was up, and Clyde was running late. He and Methvin took turns during the night to stay awake and keep watch. Clyde spotted a police car slowly driving towards him, using the middle-of-the-road, so as not to get stuck. When the car stopped, and the two officers got out, Clyde started to back his car up. Clyde hoped it would be a clean getaway, but the car's rear wheels sank deep in mud, which forced the car into the ditch.

The officers pulled their handguns first and, for no apparent reason, started firing at the Ford. Clyde and Methvin got out of the Ford and returned fire with the BAR rifles. Campbell died instantly, and Boyd was only nicked. Clyde took him prisoner, and this time gave Methvin specific instructions that he was not to be killed.

The story goes on to say; there was a farmhouse nearby. Three men emerged from the house to check out all the noise. Clyde ordered them to help push his Ford out of the ditch. However, the men could not free the car. By this time, a couple of other cars had stopped close to the action to see what was going on. To their surprise, Clyde moved towards them with his Bar rifle and ordered them over to help push. The Barrow car remained in the ditch. Then a heavy truck came on the scene. Clyde ordered the driver to pull the Ford out with a chain. With his car back on the road, Clyde thanked the men for their help. Before getting into the car, Clyde told the men they had just met Bonnie and Clyde. He wished them a pleasant day and took off in the Ford.

With Boyd, their prisoner, Clyde put as many miles between him and Commerce as he could. During the trip, they gave Boyd, food, clean clothes, but did not steal his money. It was reported that Boyd felt sorry for Bonnie, who was almost totally crippled. In the end, Clyde let Boyd go, and the chief made his way back to Commerce on April 7, 1934.

Chapter 12
Bonnie and Clyde's Days are numbered

After letting Boyd go, Clyde over the next few days knocked off another couple of banks and a few stores. Then Bonnie, Clyde and Methvin headed back to the Dallas area. The pair had not seen their families since March 1934. Bonnie was anxious to see her mother and give her Sonny Boy, the Easter rabbit. Bonnie joked with Clyde that Sonny Boy was becoming famous. In just the last three weeks, he had been involved in two gunfights, which left three lawmen dead. The rabbit was also involved in three bank robberies, the hold-up of several stores and filling stations. She told Clyde, I will have to make sure mama keeps him hidden from the law, or he will end up at Eastham, referring to the prison farm. Clyde looked at Bonnie and mentioned Eastham; he will end up on someone's plate as a fried rabbit.

The Barrow Gang finally met with their families and exchanged the latest information and stories. The atmosphere was tense, as Hamer was giving interviews to newspapers about hunting down Bonnie and Clyde. The family members realized he had been a famous Texas Ranger and was known for getting his prey. Some members of the family suggested that Bonnie and Clyde should head for Mexico, where they could find safety. However, the pair wanted to remain in the States so that they could visit their families.

The newspapers were now publishing articles about Frank Hamer and his legendary pursuit of the outlaws. Bonnie and Clyde were aware of Hamer being on their trail. The date was now mid-April 1934, and tension was running high with both families. They did not talk about the end much, but everyone knew and understood the end was probably close. They were also aware that Hamer preferred to take his prey dead.

For the next few weeks, Clyde stayed close to Dallas. He also believed he had a true friend in Henry Methvin. Little did he know that Henry and his old man made a deal to lure them into a deadly ambush? Clyde made a trip to Louisiana near the end of April. It was a one-day trip, not enough time for the posse to act. Near the end of April, Clyde also drove to Joplin, Missouri, to finish some business with an outlaw friend. At about the same time, Clyde learned that Ray Hamilton had been arrested. Clyde then travelled to Memphis, Tennessee, where he robbed the Farmer's Trust and Savings Bank. His haul from the bank was a tidy sum of $1600. However, Bonnie and Clyde had no vision, spiritual or otherwise that this would be the last bank they would ever rob.

In making their escape, Clyde drove off in what can only be described as the most elegant car he ever stole. It was a beautiful new Ford V8 sedan, which he stole from the driveway of Ruth and Jesse Warren of Topeka,

Kansas, on April 29, 1934. Again, Bonnie and Clyde had no vision that this would be the last automobile they would ever steal. The law was on their heels, and the most famous manhunt of all time was quickly coming to an end.

The following description is supposedly how Clyde came to acquire this car.

On April 29, 1934, Ruth had the car out for a leisurely afternoon drive. On returning home, she parked the car in her driveway and left the keys in the ignition. (Leaving the keys in the car is something most of us would never do today, but back in those days, it was a common occurrence.) She went into the house, and her husband was down the street, visiting his mother.

It would be three months before Ruth Warren would see the bullet-ridden car again with a blood-soaked interior. By this time, the car had become famous, as it was the automobile in which Bonnie and Clyde died in.

The following day, after Bonnie and Clyde drove off in the car, Kansas State Police reported that a vehicle fitting the description of the Warren vehicle had been seen. Police stationed in Ottawa, Kansas, about 40 miles from Topeka, reported seeing a car of the same description with out-of-state license plates. The report said it was parked behind a hedgerow for most of Sunday in the late afternoon and evening. The following day, state police visited the scene. Officers found fresh tire tracks, cigar butts and a telltale clue, which alerted them that it was Bonnie and Clyde. Bonnie had left a pair of her panties lying on the ground with a red rose inside them. Bonnie, a seasoned promoter of the Barrow Gang, would deliberately leave intimate clues behind to frustrate the police.

The State Police remained on the alert over the entire mid-south and mid-central states for the tan-coloured Ford, but it was not spotted. Clyde was known for driving long distances at night as he was fast and an expert driver. The police were well aware that Barrow liked V-8 Fords. The cars got good gas mileage and could travel at high speeds over long distances, without breaking down. It was a common car and blended in well with highway traffic, for someone who wanted to remain anonymous on the highway.

The calendar now turned over to May 1934. It would be intriguing to know what was going through Bonnie's mind. Thanks to Bonnie, keeping a diary of their adventures, we now have a lasting insight into what she was thinking. It was clear, by the beginning of May 1934, Bonnie was sensing impending death. Her diary notes were an eerie tale of gloom and doom. Death was closing in on her, and she was ready to accept it. Then in the final days, she put up a struggle to convince Clyde to bale immediately.

As April 1934 ended, the lawmen involved in finding Bonnie and Clyde were under public ridicule of their clumsy efforts to catch the couple. Newspapers mocked Sheriff Schmid. Cartoon punch lines told of Bonnie and Clyde giving Schmid, twelve hours to get out of town or else. Schmid was up for re-election, and if he didn't get support, his public office days were over. He was hoping to bathe in some of the glory for catching Bonnie and Clyde.

However, they did not call Frank Hamer the most famous Texas Ranger for nothing. To visit the Methvin family, Clyde had to travel over narrow, lonely bush roads. These roads were mostly lined with thick bush on each side. Hamer was thinking about an old fashion western ambush in a secluded place. To accomplish this, Hamer had to lure Bonnie and Clyde into a false sense of security.

Hamer deliberately made an all-out effort to make himself and his posse visible in the states of Missouri, Oklahoma, Texas, Kansas and Arkansas. Hamer and Jordan had secretly picked out what they considered the best ambush locations on roads leading into Bienville Parish. Hamer was successful in securing two BAR rifles to be used in the ambush. For Hamer, the plan to ambush Bonnie and Clyde on a lonely back road was coming together. All he was missing was a time and place.

The gang made a trip to Louisiana. They kept their visits short and their schedule a secret. While Henry was visiting his parents, Bonnie and Clyde were out driving the back roads of Louisiana. In her diary, Bonnie states, Clyde was trying to pick out a place, where they might eventually settle down. At night, the couple camped out, sometimes as far as 80 miles from the Methvin home.

Clyde left Louisiana suddenly on May 6, 1934, and drove to Dallas for a get together with their families. Bonnie was in a brooding mood with her family. She insisted on going over plans she had come up with, her mother. Emma tried to change the subject, but Bonnie was determined. She told her mother, her death was imminent, and she needed to talk.

On this visit, Bonnie gave her mother what many believe was her last poem. Bonnie called the poem "The End of the Line." However, it has become known as "The Story of Bonnie and Clyde." This was not her last poem. In her diary, she has a poem dated May 10, 1934, called "Retribution." The poem is near the end of this book.

Bonnie and Clyde only stayed for a couple of hours, promising to return in a few weeks for another visit. Two nights later, Clyde showed up at his family's home late at night without Bonnie. This was not unusual for Clyde. However, this time he asked his father to meet him, a short distance from their home. Henry Barrow followed Clyde's instructions and met with him.

At this point, there are different versions of what took place. Because of that, it is now impossible to know what actually happened. The following is probably close to what took place.

Clyde asked his father (Henry) to meet him a short distance from the family home. The reason for this meeting was to have his father sign some papers, which were supposedly instructions for Clyde's Will. Henry was illiterate, so there was no way for him to know if it actually was a Will.

According to Bonnie's diary, Henry did sign the papers. At the time, Henry noticed, his son's suitcase containing the Will was full of money. After Henry signed the Will, Clyde told him that he and Bonnie were making plans to relocate both their families. The move would be a long way from Dallas, where the law would not bother them. Just how much information Clyde told his father will never be known. Before leaving, Clyde told his father he would return in a few weeks and with that, he said good-bye.

There was speculation that Clyde may have had as much as $20,000 in the suitcase. The story suggests that Clyde was planning to free O.D. Stevens from the Tarrant County jail. This man was an important part of the criminal underworld, and he was desperate to get out of jail. The Eastham prison caper by Bonnie and Clyde raised their value to the underworld. Clyde started to get credit for other prison breaks even though he had nothing to do with them. Stevens knew about Clyde's reputation and figured if anyone could do it, he could. The speculation was the money Clyde had in the suitcase was a partial payment for breaking Stevens out of jail.

Through the second and third weeks in May 1934, Bonnie and Clyde were spending most of their time in Bienville Parish. Clyde was now flush with money and was not robbing. Hamer had told Jordan to leave Clyde alone, so he would feel safe and possibly make an error in judgment.

The posse was ready and waiting for the right moment to put their ambush plan into action. While they were waiting, Bonnie and Clyde were enjoying Louisiana hospitality, Methvin style. Henry and his father were about to betray Clyde, but other Methvin relatives were treating them like movie stars. The Barrow couple was enjoying the attention. Clyde hadn't seen any lawmen, and that made the affair even more enjoyable. However, things can be misleading, and Clyde was probably letting his guard down, just a little.

By the middle of May 1934, Hamer was fed up with waiting to hear from Sheriff Jordan. He took the Texas part of the posse and headed for Louisiana. They would now take the hunt to Bonnie and Clyde.

The Barrow Gang headed out Monday morning, May 21, to Shreveport. Clyde had a couple of errands to run, and by the time he finished, it was noon. He stopped at the Majestic Cafe, and Henry went inside to pick up sandwiches and something to drink. A police cruiser drove by the cafe while Henry was inside. As a precaution, Bonnie and Clyde drove off. They made a few circles of the town, and then returned to the cafe to pick Henry up. However, Henry noticed Clyde driving away, and he left the cafe without the order and headed back to Bienville Parish by himself. Clyde went into the cafe and picked up the order. He returned to the car and headed for a remote location out of town, where they ate their lunch and rested for a while.

Meanwhile, Hamer, with three members of his posse and a fourth unknown member, checked into a hotel in Shreveport. On Monday afternoon, Hamer contacted the local police chief to let them know, Lawmen from another jurisdiction were in town on official business. The police chief knew about Hamer's posse and mentioned that two of his officers may have sighted Clyde, in a Ford V8 car that was parked in town. The chief told Hamer the circumstances, and Hamer recognized Clyde's pattern.

Hamer visited the Majestic Cafe in the afternoon and got a positive ID on Henry Methvin. The waitress looked at mug shots and picked out Henry. Hamer then drove 55 miles south to Arcadia, where he met with Jordan. After reviewing the information, Hamer decided to set up an ambush. He chose the most likely road leading to Methvin's place, which was the Sailes Jamestown road 154. Weeks earlier, they had selected a location, so it was just a matter of driving to the location, hiding their vehicles and hunkering down for the kill. Hamer figured, with a little luck, he might be able to bag his prey the next day.

Jordan told Hamer, he would need to find Ivy Methvin, as he was the bait. Jordan then told the Texans, they could return to their hotel rooms in Shreveport, and keep out of sight. He told them, Arcadia is a small gossip town, and word would surely get back to Bonnie and Clyde. Hamer saw the logic in the argument and returned to Shreveport.

At this point, in the story, there are several versions of what took place. Therefore, it is now impossible to establish how things went down.

One story has the Barrow Gang meeting with the Methvins on May 21, at a place called Black Lake. It was thought Clyde might stay there for the night, but he didn't. Apparently, on Tuesday, May 22, Bonnie and Clyde drove down the road, which they would be killed on the next day. They were on that road driving to Methvin's place to get Henry. He was not at home, and Henry's father told Clyde that Henry would be there the next morning. He told Clyde to show up the following day at nine, which would be Wednesday, May 23, 1934. It played out that way, so Bonnie and Clyde must have felt okay with the circumstances.

Henry's father was pressing Jordan to ambush Clyde on Tuesday. Reports show Jordan was trying to contact a specific government agent. The government was hoping to share in some of the credit for the shooting of Bonnie and Clyde. If this is true, then Jordan gave the Barrows an extra day to live.

Ivy Methvin got in touch with Jordan and promised him that Bonnie and Clyde would be driving down that road, the next morning around 9:00 am. Jordan got in touch with Hamer in Shreveport and told him it was time to set up. The two parties met at Arcadia and drove to the pre-selected spot around 3:00 am. Wednesday morning. The posse and the freelance photographer selected their spots and began their wait.

Jordan told Ivy Methvin to meet him at the spot around 5:00 am Wednesday morning. From that point, Methvin was told to park his old truck in the southbound lane and jack it up. Ivy then removed a front tire to show he had trouble. Jordan then told Ivy he would have to wave Bonnie and Clyde down. Hopefully, the couple would stop or slow enough to give the posse a chance to shoot. Ivy Methvin was nervous about the plan, but Jordan told him that was the only way Texas would pardon his son, Henry. Ivy agreed to do it, but told Jordan; he needed time to take cover. The two came up with a story to tell Clyde.

The posse started to complain when they got out there. The bugs were hungry, the guns were heavy, the bush was thick, and the night was dark. Hamer kept thinking about the old west. This was going to be the real thing, and before the day was over, he would have his prey and trophy. Hamer was confident before the day was over; he would be able to hand Bonnie and Clyde's heads on a silver platter to Simmons. As the hours ticked off, the posse members became nervous and fidgety. Each lawman was going over in his mind how things would go down.

They all knew Clyde could drive and shoot his way out of seemingly impossible situations. That was evident from the Joplin and Dexfield shootouts, where the law figured they had him. Bob Alcorn and Ted Hinton knew from experience that Clyde was quite capable of driving away from a roadside ambush. Clyde was a master gunman and driver.

As the posse waited, the hours dragged by. The morning was humid, and the men were soon uncomfortable. At 5:00 am, Ivy Methvin drove up in his old Chevy truck, and Jordan gave him instructions. Methvin parked it in the southbound lane and jacked up the front end. He then pulled the left front tire off and laid it on the ground in front of the truck. He then had to sit with the posse. Each time a vehicle drove by, he had to clamour down the embankment and tell the occupants, he didn't need help. As Methvin sat with the posse, he grumbled and complained. Finally, Jordan told him to shut up, or he would shoot him. Everyone was jumpy, and there was no relief from those damn mosquitoes.

Chapter 13
Bonnie & Clyde Have Two Hours Left to Live.

The following chapter is a dramatization of what probably happened from the time Bonnie and Clyde awoke on the morning of May 23, 1934, until they pulled out of Gibsland, to meet their fate a few miles south.

As dawn broke over Louisiana, on Wednesday morning, May 23, 1934, events were being played out in three separate locations. These locations were cantered on a small community called Gibsland, Louisiana. Gibsland was a sleepy town, where nothing important ever happened. However, before this day would end, the small community would be making news headlines across the United States. In three hours, a posse of six well-armed lawmen would come face-to-face with Bonnie and Clyde. This was going to happen on a deserted section of road about eight miles south of Gibsland. The outcome had already been written in the stars. The ambush was well planned, and now it was a waiting game.

As members of the posse lay in wait, they were huddled under blankets trying to ward off mosquitoes. The men could fight the humid air, but those damn mosquitoes were enough to drive a person insane. Finally, there was a hint of light in the eastern sky, it was beginning to brighten, and dawn was breaking. One member of the posse was posted as a lookout. His immediate job was to alert the others if he saw a car coming down the small hill in the distance.

About the same time, a middle-aged woman was getting out of bed at her home in Gibsland. She owned a small cafe in the town called Ma Canfield's Cafe. It was midweek and just another workday for her. The time was 6:30 am, and she had an hour to get herself ready before taking the short walk to open her cafe.

The third event was taking place about ten miles north of Gibsland. The night before, Clyde had pulled the Ford into a wooded area off the main road. He felt comfortable that he and Bonnie would not be disturbed at that location. Now that dawn had broken, Clyde was moving around outside the car. The two had slept in the car overnight. It wasn't the most comfortable place to sleep, but at least, they didn't have to battle the mosquitoes all night.

Clyde opened the back door and shook Bonnie by the leg. She responded by opening her eyes and asking him what time it was. Clyde crawled into the back seat and closed the door. He put his hands under the blanket and began to massage her legs. Bonnie moaned as they played with each other for twenty minutes.

They finished getting dressed and splashed some water on their faces. Bonnie pulled her mirror out and started to comb her hair. Clyde told Bonnie, "We can both have a shower and a sound sleep tonight at Henry's place," referring to where they were headed. Bonnie then replied, "It's hard being on the run all the time, and in six months, I'm going to have a baby." Clyde leaned against the side of the car, and for the first time, suggested they move to a part of the country, where they could settle down in one place. Bonnie looked at Clyde and with her bubbly personality, and asked him if he meant that. He told her, "I sure do because I'm getting tired of being on the run. Buck is dead, and the law is turning up the heat on our families."

He told Bonnie if we don't get away from this life soon, the law is going to kill us. Bonnie looked deep into Clyde's eyes and saw fear in them. She told Clyde, I have a dreadful feeling about today. Let's turn this car around and get out of here; something terrible is going to happen. Clyde held her tightly and told her, maybe your right, but we are close to Henry's place. Let's rest there for a couple of days and decide where we should go. Bonnie kissed him and said, okay, let's do that, but in the meantime, let's not take any chances, I have a bad feeling. Clyde agreed and reminded Bonnie, no one other than Henry and his father knows where we are. Bonnie spoke up and said, "what if they rat on us." Clyde said they would not do that. Then Bonnie, who was familiar with the outlaws of the old American west, reminded Clyde about Bob Ford, who turned on Jesse James for a pardon.

Clyde looked at Bonnie and told her, "You are starting to spook me." We need to stay calm and get to Henry's place. We'll rest for a couple of days, then get in touch with our families and set our sights on Oregon or Washington or maybe even Canada. Bonnie looked at her watch; it was now 7:30 am. Let's get out of here and get to Henry's.

It was clear something had come over, Bonnie. She was three months pregnant, and it may have been her motherly instinct that was taking over. She needed to protect herself and her child. It also seems Clyde was feeling more and more boxed in. His brother Buck was dead, and the law was hot on his trail was one of the questions haunting him. Could Bonnie be right, would one of the remaining members of his gang betray him for immunity? Clyde thought back to yesterday, when Henry did not come back after telling them, he was going to get a sandwich and a drink. Clyde was wondering if the police had caught him.

They climbed into the front seat of the Ford, and Clyde placed a browning rifle between him and Bonnie. That was a standard procedure for Clyde. He drove the car out of the woods onto the secondary road. Down the road, a quarter-of-a-mile, he made a right turn onto the main road and headed for Gibsland.

Back in Gibsland, the time was 7:30 am, and the woman had just opened the cafe. The first thing she did was put on a pot of coffee and got some muffins out of the freezer. Next, she fried five eggs that would be made into breakfast sandwiches. Once ready, she wrapped and put them in a display case, where the bread would stay fresh. The time was now 8:14 am, and in came her first customer. The woman's name was Betty, and every morning at this time, she would come in for a coffee and muffin.

Back eight miles south of Gibsland, the six lawmen were talking, grumbling and fighting off the mosquitoes. The sun had come up, and the men had a perfect view of the Hwy northbound. A little known fact about the posse was they had the seventh man with them. His job was to film the whole event, starting from when they would first spot the Barrow car.

Bonnie and Clyde were now entering Gibsland, and Clyde pulled over to park near Ma Canfield's Cafe. The couple wanted to get some breakfast. The time was 8:20 am. Clyde got out of the car and entered the cafe. He ordered breakfast to go and purchased a newspaper and a fashion magazine for Bonnie. When he returned to the car, he ate his breakfast.

Chapter 14
The Bonnie and Clyde Ambush,
as the world has known it for the past 75 years

Finally, about 9:15 in the morning, the posse heard the unmistakable sound of a powerful engine coming from the north. The tan-coloured Ford V8 came into view on the now-famous curved hill, about a quarter-mile away. Inside the car, Clyde was driving in his stocking feet. Bonnie was slowly eating her sandwich as she looked through the magazine Clyde has bought for her.

Hinton estimated the Ford was travelling as fast as 50 mph as it was closing the distance quickly. As the car got closer, Hinton made the call; it was Bonnie and Clyde. Alcorn agreed, and the word went down-the-line.

As the car got closer, it slowed down. The posse parked Henry Melvin's old truck in the southbound lane across from their hiding spot. They had pulled the front tire off to make it look as if it had a flat tire. The Barrow car was getting closer. The posse members raised their guns in a ready position. Jordan signalled old man Methvin to flag Clyde down.

As Clyde approached the old truck, he recognized it and saw Methvin standing beside it. Clyde came to a full stop in the northbound lane beside the truck. Methvin said something to Clyde, then turned and made a dive for cover under his truck. Within a split second, two or three shots were fired. About three seconds later, the deafening roar of six guns opened fire on the Barrow car in the morning silence. Clyde had shifted into low gear as he came to a stop. With the life drained out of him, his left foot slipped off the clutch, and the car lurched forward as the motor died. The ambush was over in thirty seconds. Clyde never had a chance to grab his rifle. The first shots fired by Oakley blew the back of Clyde's head off. The inside of the car was splattered with human blood, flesh and brains. Clyde was slumped against the door, and Bonnie was slumped against him. With life in their bodies only seconds before, they were now corpses. The outlaw reign of Bonnie and Clyde was over.

In the end, Clyde's car had rolled about fifty feet forward and came to rest in the shallow ditch. The posse approached the vehicle cautiously, as Clyde had more lives than a dead cat. However, with one look inside the car, all they saw were two shot-up bodies. Old man Methvin crawled out from underneath his truck and asked the men from the posse to help him get his wheel back on the truck. They ignored him. In the end, he put the wheel on himself and drove away as the cowardly man he was.

Just before the shooting started, an old logging truck had stopped on the side of the road in the northbound lane. With the shooting over, the logging truck's driver and passenger slowly approached the death scene. The members of the posse then emptied the car of its treasures, which were Clyde's tools of his trade.

Ted Hinton produced a 16-millimetre movie camera. He started filming the death scene, the corpses and the weapons. The lawmen had trouble hearing one another. The deafening roar of the gunfire caused the posse temporary hearing impairment.

Lee Simmons, the Texas prison general manager, had promised Hamer that he could have anything, which Clyde had in his possession at the time of his death. Hamer, who now had his prize trophy, was quickly taking inventory of the car's contents.

The contents of the car included:

=== Five Browning automatic rifles (BARS)
        and 6 sets of clips.
=== Two sawed-off shotguns, a 12 gauge and a 20 gauge.|
=== Several other shotguns and rifles.
=== Fifteen handguns, a colt 32 calibre, a colt 45 calibre
        and several colt automatic pistols.
=== One ten gauge Winchester lever action.
=== About 3,000 rounds of ammunition.
=== Fifteen sets of stolen license plates.
=== Four suitcases full of clothes.
=== One suite case full of money
=== One lady's makeup case.
=== One fishing tackle box.
=== Several true crime magazines.
=== Various road maps.
=== One saxophone.
=== An envelope with information about Canada.
=== A pink and white baby dress and a small doll.

Hamer took all the weapons, ammo, and the tackle box. The other lawmen had to be content with the minor souvenirs. Bob Alcorn, who took Clyde's saxophone, later returned it to Clyde's mother for peace of mind. The suitcase full of money disappeared, and the Barrow family believed it was the work of Henderson Jordan because he purchased land in Arcadia not long after the ambush.

With the treasure divvied up and locked safely in the lawmen's cars, it was time to get the messy part of the ambush, cleaned up. Oakley, Gault, and Alcorn stayed behind to guard the Ford and the bodies while the other three drove back to Gibsland. The Bienville Parish coroner in Arcadia was contacted and told to drive out to the ambush site. A towing company was called as a tow truck was needed for the Ford.

Hinton called Smoot Schmid and told him to contact the press. Schmid, after contacting the news, drove to Louisiana to get some credit. Hamer called Lee Simmons and told him Bonnie and Clyde died with guns in their hands. The three lawmen in their excitement didn't realize their conversations were overheard by locals milling around. Word soon got around that Bonnie and Clyde were dead in their car just south of town. Within minutes Hwy 154 heading south of town became a road filled with a procession of cars, bikes, trucks and people on foot. The lawmen, after notifying all the bosses, headed back to the ambush site but had to contend with a circus of vehicles and people all heading south.

When they arrived back at the site, a crowd of people had already gathered. The gunfire was so loud, it was heard by locals up to three miles away. These people made their way to the location to see what had happened. While some were trying to get a look inside the car, many others were frantically trying to grab anything they could as souvenirs. The three lawmen left behind, could not fully control the crowd. Some of the sightseers managed to reach inside the Ford and cut off pieces of Bonnie's dress, strands of her hair and pieces of the car seat. When the other three lawmen returned, order was quickly restored, and the crowd was kept at bay.

The tow truck finally arrived, and the Ford was chained to it. The coroner made a preliminary observation, and then the car, with the remains still inside it, was towed to Arcadia. Oakley and Jordan's car led the way, followed by the tow truck and the other two lawmen's cars. Behind all that was a line up of private vehicles, which stretched back close to a mile.

While all this was going on, the wire service in the United States had picked up the story. The news was quickly spreading across the country. The powerful crime syndicate bosses, now realized, with the brutal killing of Bonnie and Clyde, their days were numbered.

As the tow truck made its way to Arcadia, the worst possible scenario happened. The wrecker broke down in front of the Gibsland public school, just as many of the students were starting their recess.

The school children quickly swarmed around the tow truck and the car, as word spread the bodies of Bonnie and Clyde were in the car. The bodies had been covered with a sheet, but one of the kids reached in and pulled the sheet out of the vehicle. All eyes could now see the mutilated corpses. One of the students (Polly Palmer) in an interview over sixty years later described how Bonnie's lip was almost severed from her mouth. Another wrecker finally arrived, but the damage was already done. The ghastly scene would haunt many children for the rest of their lives.

The second wrecker towed the Ford to Arcadia, where the local population of 3,500 had swelled to estimates of 12,000. The funeral parlour staff tried to remove the bodies from the car and put them on gurneys, but the public turned into savages. They were pushing and shoving one another while trying to grab the bodies and pull off anything they could get as souvenirs. The most common comment circulating among the public was how small the two criminals were. One fellow remarked, "Clyde looked like a little tiny fart." A second man commented that Clyde was no bigger than a schoolboy. People were taking pictures, and the crowd was getting out of control. Jordan fired his gun in the air several times and told the people to get back, or else, the funeral home would have more bodies to bury.

During those years, the funeral home was located in the backroom of Conger's Furniture Store. The bodies of Bonnie and Clyde were removed from the car and taken into the funeral home. The coroner held a hasty inquest. He examined the bodies and listed the details. Bonnie had a tattoo on the inside of her right thigh. All the gunshot wounds were listed. The cause of death was identified as several gunshot wounds. Bob Alcorn formally identified the deceased. Somehow, a newspaper reporter managed to get in the examining room and snapped pictures of the two naked bodies. He took pictures of them as they lay on the embalming tables. The pictures were distributed to newspapers and magazines and published. Hamer didn't care about the pictures but was satisfied at how the public viewed the law's revenge on the Barrow gang. When the bodies were clothed, the public was invited to file past the two legendary outlaws as they lay on tables. The autopsy indicated, Bonnie had 51 gunshot wounds, while Clyde had 31 wounds. The car had over 150 bullet holes in it.

As reporters arrived in Arcadia, the town took on a festival-like atmosphere. Hamer told the press that both Bonnie and Clyde had reached for guns before the posse opened fire. Rumours started circulating that a local citizen was the informant, and all eyes turned to Ivy Methvin, but the law did not say anything. The events of the ambush were straight forward, yet different posse members gave their own version of what happened.

Henry Barrow and his son Jack travelled to Arcadia to claim Clyde's body, while Bonnie's brother Buster arrived to claim Bonnie's body. The families learned of the deaths when newspaper reporters called to get comments. Bonnie's mother fainted on hearing the news. The families contacted different funeral homes in Dallas, to arrange for transportation of the bodies back to Dallas. Bonnie's mother, Emma, told family and friends, that Clyde had Bonnie in life, but would not have her in death. Now that Bonnie was dead, Emma did not pretend that she liked Clyde anymore.

With Bonnie and Clyde dead, the families were hoping that the public interest would diminish. However, the public had a thirst for any scrap of information they could read, including the funerals. Both families made a terrible decision by allowing open visitation at the funeral homes. They estimated 10,000 people filed past Clyde's body, and the police had to be called in to restore order. Bonnie's visitation attracted about 20,000 people, but things went reasonably well.

Clyde's funeral was on Friday afternoon, May 25, 1934, and he was buried in the Western Heights Cemetery in Dallas. He shared a grave with his brother Buck. The crowd was so thick; the pallbearers had trouble carrying Clyde's body to the gravesite.

Bonnie's funeral was on Saturday, May 26, 1934, and she was buried in the Fish Trap Cemetery. Her gravesite was beside her niece and nephew, who died eight months earlier. The police provided more crowd control, but they estimated even more people were at the cemetery for Bonnie than Clyde. Bonnie predicted in one of her poems that she would die with Clyde, and it came true. However, Bonnie could never have imagined the mythology that would grow about her and Clyde. Today, more than three-quarters of a century after their deaths, their legend is larger than life. People are trying to figure out what exactly happened to make Bonnie and Clyde so famous. Of all the criminals in the United States past and present, Bonnie and Clyde are by far the most famous. In 1945, Bonnie Parker, her niece and nephew, were reburied in the Crown Hill Memorial Park Cemetery in Dallas, beside Emma Parker.

Life after Bonnie and Clyde

The ambush of Bonnie and Clyde in May 1934 was just the beginning. The United States Congress passed several crime bills. These bills were designed to give J. Edgar Hoover and his Division of Investigation agents more authority. Bank robbing became a federal crime and thieves could no longer hide, by travelling from one state to another.

U.S. agents killed John Dillinger on July 22, 1934. Pretty Boy Floyd met his death on October 22, and Baby Face Nelson was gunned down on November 27. On January 16, 1935, Ma Barker and her son Fred were killed. The ambush of Bonnie and Clyde proved to be the beginning of the end for the "public enemy era" of the 1930s.

Chapter 15
The Bonnie & Clyde Ambush,
from the memoirs of the unknown seventh man

In 1985, I (the author) met the seventh man, who was with the posse when Bonnie and Clyde were ambushed. His name was Charles Baker, and he was a distant relative. He had filmed the event, including the car approaching, the gunfire and everything else, which happened afterwards. His filming ended, when the Death Car was towed away with Bonnie and Clyde still inside. Frank Hamer hired Baker as a free-lance photographer. Hamer, at the time, wanted the event captured on film for his own use. Hamer probably chose Baker because the former Texas Ranger had used him on two other occasions, involving police work and trusted him.

In 1985, Charles Baker had cancer and would succumb to the disease before the end of the year. On that May weekend in 1985, when he visited my parent's home, he noticed a book on my mother's coffee table about Bonnie and Clyde. As he looked through it, he passed the remark, "I remember this as if it happened yesterday." I was reading the book earlier in the day and had set it on the table when my eyes became tired.

Charles then asked my father if he knew about Charles's involvement with the Bonnie and Clyde ambush. My father answered yes and said, "He was told about it back in 1936 by Charles' father." Charles then said, "What you don't know is the story, which has been told all these years was not exactly what happened." Charles then told us that he had cancer and was not expected to live past the end of the year. He also told us that he was forbidden to talk about the Bonnie and Clyde ambush to anyone or else. However, Charles did tell his parents, and subsequently, they told a couple of close relatives, one of which was my father.

That happened over 50 years ago, and now all six men of the posse are dead. The truth has never come out, and Charles has no idea what happened to the film that he shot. He told us, he is now the only remaining witness to what took place that morning in May 1934. He believes it would be wrong to go to his grave and take the truth with him.

Charles then turned and asked me if I would be able to keep what he was about to say, a secret until the year 2010. I answered, yes. He then asked me to swear that I would keep the following conversation and information secret until the year 2010.

With that out-of-the-way, I asked him why 2010. He said there are two reasons. The first one being, by that time, more than three-quarters of a century will have passed. That should be enough time that all those involved will be dead. Hopefully, their relatives will be mature enough to learn the truth without repercussions to anyone. By 2010, the world will be a different place, and the events of the early 1930s will be colourful reading of historical events.

The second reason was Bonnie, in writing her last poem, mentions the year 2010, as the year her and Clyde are released from hell. They can then join their families in a far better place. Charles told me, Bonnie's last poem was one of the items he would be mailing to me when he returns home. Charles then went on to tell us about the ambush of Bonnie and Clyde.

When he left to return to his home, I asked my father if what he was telling us was true. My father told me, Charles was the photographer hired by Hamer, to film the event, and I have known that since 1936. As for all the other details he has told us, I have no reason not to believe him. He is dying, and I think he wants to go with a clean conscience.

Charles Baker was the forgotten seventh man at the ambush site. He was hired by Frank Hamer to film the events as they unfolded. Hamer, in days gone by, was a famous Texas Ranger. He understood the importance of using the latest technology to capture what was about to happen.

Baker had three movie cameras set up and ready to roll, as soon as the tan Ford came into view. The now-famous curve on the hill was about a quarter-mile away from where the posse was hiding. When the car came into view, Baker had his cameras rolling. They stayed on until the death car was ready to be towed to Arcadia. The agreement was Baker would turn all film over to Frank Hamer, and he would never talk to anyone about what he witnessed. Baker stayed true to the agreement until 1985. At that point in time, he told me (the author) it would be wrong to die and not pass on what I witnessed that day.

What Charles Baker filmed that Morning

On the morning of the ambush, May 23, 1934, Charles Baker was positioned to the left of Hamer, at the south end of the posse line. He had all his camera equipment set up and ready to roll. Hamer, who was an experienced bounty hunter, recognized the importance of having the whole event captured on film. Hinton had brought a film camera with him, but Hamer did not want to take any chances of a screwup and hired his own photographer.

Just before 9:10 in the morning, a tan-coloured Ford V8 appeared at the top of the north hill. The car slowed and came to a stop. It remained there for about five minutes and then started down the hill. Baker believes that was probably an early sign that Bonnie and Clyde were in the car. During the time they were stopped on the hill, Bonnie and Clyde must have been debating about what they saw ahead on the road. Was the truck broke down, or was it a trap?

Finally, the Ford started to move forward and was closing at a cautious speed. As the car got closer, Hinton lowered his binoculars and made the call; it was Bonnie and Clyde. Alcorn agreed, and the word went down-the-line. As the car closed to within 200 feet from Methvin's truck, the driver pulled the vehicle into the northbound lane. Hinton signalled the rest of the posse again; it was a positive ID. The two occupants in the car were Bonnie, and Clyde and they were alone. As the car approached the old truck, it slowed to a crawl.

Jordan signalled old man Methvin to wave the car down. Methvin moved from in front of the truck to the driver's side door and waved his arms. The posse was ready with guns raised. As Clyde brought the car to a stop alongside the old truck, Methvin took a couple of steps and bent over slightly to look into the car's passenger-side window. The front of the truck was facing south, and it was jacked up on the driver's side with the front wheel off. Baker could tell there was a conversation in progress, but could not hear it.

Baker had three cameras set up and rolling. One camera was no more than ten feet away from the side of the car and was located low to the ground. The camera lens was looking directly at Clyde. The second camera was located on Hamer's right side, about four feet off the ground. Baker was filming with the third camera just to the left of Hamer.

The two occupants inside the car were Bonnie and Clyde. For a few seconds, Clyde spoke with Methvin. Baker said, "He could not hear the conversation." Suddenly, two or three shots rang out, and Clyde's head smashed against the steering wheel. Bonnie started to scream, and old man Methvin made a dive for cover under his truck.

There was no further shooting, but Bonnie's screaming was so loud and intense that it must have frozen the posse for a few seconds. Baker himself was literally shaking. Bonnie began yelling at the posse that she was pregnant and was giving up. She repeated herself three times. She yelled, "Clyde is dead." She was begging them not to shoot her. Her motherly instincts must have kicked in, as she was trying to protect her unborn child. But, it was not to be.

As she was yelling at the posse, Clyde was indeed dead, for his feet slipped off the brake and the clutch. This caused the car to jerk forward, and then it rolled ever so slowly forward.

A few more seconds passed, and Baker believed the lawmen were going to take Bonnie alive. Then in the blink of an eye, the guns opened up, and all hell broke loose. The posse began firing with everything they had on a defenceless crippled woman. Bonnie's screaming was drowned out. The noise was deafening, as the automatic guns emptied their shells into the side of the car. One could see glass shattering. The force of so many bullets hitting the car with that intensity caused smoke, and the car continued rolling. Clyde's head was now slumped backwards. For a few seconds, you could see both bodies being tossed around like rag dolls, and then Bonnie disappeared from view. She obviously slumped forward below the visibility of the windshield.

The noise of shells hitting the car caused pain to everyone's ears. Smoke began to rise from the car, and Baker thought it was on fire. The shells continued hitting the car, and finally, the guns went silent. Baker admitted, he was shaking so much, he had trouble walking for a bit. Baker also admitted, he had nightmares for several years after, about the shooting and seeing the two bodies being tossed around inside the car. He wished that he had never taken the assignment.

The car had rolled to a stop on the east side of the road in front of Hamer. The ex-Ranger called out to his men to hold their position, as he cautiously made his way down to the front of the car. Standing in front of the car, he raised his gun and fired several rounds into the passenger's side of the front windshield. Before Hamer fired at the windshield, Baker could not see Bonnie. Hamer then walked up to the passenger-side window and looked in. He then moved to the back end of the car and shouted at the other men to come down as Bonnie and Clyde were dead.

Whether Hamer was going to give Bonnie and Clyde fair warning before the shooting started will never be known. Oakley jumped the gun and fired prematurely, killing Clyde.

The one thing Baker could not comprehend was the fact; they could have taken Bonnie alive, but chose not to. In the weeks following that horrible scene, Baker had nightmares about Bonnie and the savage way she died. Clyde never knew what hit him, but Bonnie had precious seconds to think about it.

The story is told, the lawmen pumped over 150 shells into the side of the car. Many of those shells hit Bonnie and Clyde. That story was told over and over, books were written, and movies were made about it. It became the most legendary shootout in American Criminal History. On that lonely Louisiana road in May 1934, Bonnie and Clyde died that day, but "The Legend of Bonnie and Clyde," continues to live on.

Until the end of his life, Charles Baker had nightmares about what he witnessed that morning. There was one image he could never forget. That image was Bonnie's body being tossed around like a rag doll, as the shells struck it.

The whole incident was over in thirty seconds or so. Inside the car were the corpses of Bonnie and Clyde, soaked in their own blood. Baker was clearly shaken, as Bonnie had given the posse a clear signal that she was surrendering. Her speech was loud and shaky, but clear enough to be understood by Baker, who was one of the furthest from the car.

When the posse came out from their hiding spots and onto the road, Baker followed them with the film rolling. The men from the posse opened the two doors on the passenger side of the car. They then stepped back, so Baker could film the inside of the car before anything was disturbed. Baker admitted that his stomach almost turned as he looked at the bullet-riddled bodies. Blood, brains and flesh were splashed all over the inside of the car. There was blood on the outside of the car and some on the ground. Baker described it as a grizzly and hellish scene, one that would haunt him for the rest of his life.

Once Baker finished taking overall shots of the car's inside, the posse moved Clyde's body forward. They learned it against the driver's side door with the face looking up. A section of the back of Clyde's head was blown away. The expression on his face was a man in horror. They then moved Bonnie's body to an upright position and leaned it against Clydes.

Hamer told Baker to take photographs of the items in the car. The posse then removed everything from inside the car and piled it outside. Hamer then told Baker to take stills of Bonnie and Clyde and when finished to take pictures of all the items piled outside.

The Posse, Missed Bonnie's Diary

Charles Baker admitted, he found an overlooked piece of valuable information the posse missed when they were cleaning out the Death Car. It was Bonnie's diary. She had it under the front seat fastened to the upper section of it. He said it could only be spotted if one looked under the seat and upward.

After the posse had everything out of the car, they were standing around and examining Clyde's treasures. Hamer had given Baker instructions, to take pictures of Bonnie and Clyde from different angles. While doing what he was told, Baker looked under the front seat near Bonnie's leg and just happened to catch a glimpse of a book. With the posse focused on Clyde's cache, Baker reached up and pulled the book down. He opened it and realized it was Bonnie's diary. He quickly stuffed it under his jacket. He later admitted, he must have had a lapse in judgment to take such a chance. If Hamer had discovered the diary on him, God knows what would have happened.

Baker then moved back from the car a couple of feet and took a picture. He observed the men were at the back end of the vehicle, totally involved in the treasure they had just discovered. Baker walked to the front of the car, where he had left his camera bag. The camera bag had a thin removable cloth-covered board on the bottom to give it rigidity. He quickly pulled the diary from under his jacket and placed it under the board. He then grabbed a roll of film and returned to the side of the car to continue taking pictures. No one from the posse gave his movements a second glance. When his job was finished, he handed all the film over to Hamer. Hamer then asked Baker to open all the cameras. He then asked to see the inside of the camera bag. When he said that, Baker thought for sure, he would discover the diary, but he did not. When the death car was towed away, Baker's job was complete. In the following weeks, Baker read the diary and made a handwritten copy of it. However, the diary only went back to January 1, 1934. Baker concluded that Bonnie's complete diary was done in segments. Bonnie only had one in the car, which turned out to be the last one.

Two years after the ambush, Baker decided the right thing to do was give the diary to Bonnie's mother. He contacted her and explained who he was and his reason for getting in touch with her. She accepted the diary and thanked him. She also had questions for him, but he decided it was best to tell her that Bonnie died instantly with no pain. He also told her never to tell anyone where she got the diary from. Baker told her he would be breaking an agreement with Hamer. He told Bonnie's mother, if Hamer ever found out, he would be arrested and thrown in jail or even killed. She promised him his secret was safe with her. He never saw Bonnie's mother again. What she did with her daughter's diary will never be known.

It should also be noted that Hinton took pictures with his own film camera of the car, its occupants and all the guns. Baker made the statement that as far as he knows, none of his pictures he took were ever released by Hamer. Today in our modern world, we have the Internet. The site called "YouTube" does show some video footage of the Death Car and Bonnie and Clyde. There is no way of knowing who took this video. However, from a professional standpoint, the film does not look professionally shot. It, therefore, probably comes from Hinton's camera. So the question is, did Hamer destroy all the pictures that Baker took that day or are they stored away somewhere?

There are rumours and speculation that Clyde had a suitcase full of money in the car at the time of the ambush. Baker said all the items in the car were taken out, including suitcases and opened up. There was no suitcase containing money. The only money the posse found was approximately $400.00, which Clyde had on him.

Chapter 16
Highlights' of Bonnie Parker's Diary

May 23, 1934
Bonnie's last entry in her diary
Since Bonnie was killed about 9:15 am, she would have written this entry earlier that morning. The entry simply said, "I awoke this morning with a bad feeling. I believe today is my last day on this earth. I love you, mama. Please pray for me. May the Lord have mercy on my soul."

May 22, 1934
Bonnie makes reference to the fact she and Clyde travelled to Methvin's place for nothing as Henry was not there. Bonnie writes she has mixed feelings about Henry, but Clyde trusts him.

May 21, 1934
Bonnie writes that Henry skipped out after telling her and Clyde, he would get them lunch. Bonnie makes reference to the fact; she thinks he is a weasel.

May 20, 1934
Bonnie makes reference to the fact she has had another dream about the law ambushing her and Clyde on a Louisiana back road. She pleads with Clyde that they must not return to Louisiana. She makes reference that Hamer is going to kill them in an ambush.

May 19, 1934
Bonnie again writes that she wants to see her mother. She pleads with Clyde telling him she will never see her mother again if they do not go now. Clyde again tells her he is planning a trip back to Texas at the end of May.

May 18, 1934
Bonnie makes reference to the fact; she wants to lead a more normal life and settle down. According to Bonnie, Clyde is going to give up his life of robbery, murder and being on the run as soon as he completes his last mission.

May 17, 1934
Bonnie writes that she wants to see her mother. Clyde tells her he is planning a trip back to Texas at the end of May.

May 14, 1934
Bonnie writes in this entry that Clyde has the money buried in a watertight container. She makes reference to the fact, Clyde was nervous about carrying such a large sum of cash in their travels. She makes no other reference to the money.

Baker said, "The posse found about four hundred dollars cash on Clyde. The posse did not find any other money in the car. He believes the money that Bonnie mentions in her diary entry is still buried somewhere in northern Louisiana.

May 13, 1934
Bonnie makes reference that she wants to buy a new dress.

May 12, 1934
Bonnie writes that Clyde has made a special trip to check that his money is still secure.

May 11, 1934
Bonnie writes that Clyde is making a special trip tomorrow to check the spot where his money is buried. She gives no other details.

Bonnie does make reference to the fact that she is scared about dying. She senses that her and Clyde are going to be trophy material for Frank Hamer. She also writes, she fears that Hamer will follow them wherever they go.

May 10, 1934
Bonnie's last poem. This poem has insight beyond what most humans could imagine. Bonnie Parker had insight well beyond her time.

Retribution

Bonnie and Clyde were born to be lovers,
it's true in the way they lived and died.
They captured the soul of the American public,
in stories written in a paper called the Republic.

The law didn't care, about this lawless pair,
in a world filled with gloom, doom and despair.
They blasted them to hell, in a "blaze of glory,"
that will be told in a sweet police story.

They have now departed to meet their maker,
in the clear blue skies over hell's half acre.
He said, "I know the story, only too well,
and all I can offer you is a place in hell."

Bonnie said no, "please don't send us there,
send us back to Earth, for our deeds of evil"
So a deal was struck with the mighty,
A century of penance for their upheaval.

They returned to Texas under disguise,
and started their remorse in 1935.
The almighty reviewed them in 2010,
and released them early from the Eastham Pen.

Now back with their families, safe and sound,
Bonnie has a message for those on the ground.
Follow your heart, stay clean, faithful and survive,
to read about the life and times of Bonnie and Clyde.

Bonnie Parker
May 10, 1934

May 7, 1934
Bonnie tells Clyde, she has had a dream about them being ambushed on a Louisiana back road.

May 4, 1934
Bonnie writes in her diary, Today I discussed with Clyde, the message we received about meeting with the FBI. Clyde believed it was a trap and that they did not need his services. The conversation ended again on that note.

Note entered by the author

By Bonnie's entry above, it was clear the FBI made it a point to contact Bonnie and Clyde. Bonnie mentions they could use the services of Clyde. What services could Clyde offer the FBI, which they could make use of? I see only two scenarios, a trap by the FBI to capture Clyde or they do indeed need his services. The obvious answer is a trap. But, let's look at the services side of it.

What services could Clyde offer that would help the FBI? When all was said and done, Clyde does have an impressive resume. If the FBI was being sincere, it would have eliminated one bad criminal and gain a wealth of information about other criminals. Plus, they would gain a teacher who could pass on the tricks of the trade. Maybe the FBI was going to offer Bonnie and Clyde a way out to save their souls, but it's all speculation now.

A   He has a lot of contacts in the underworld.
B   All the big gangsters knew about Clyde and his reign of terror.
C   He was an expert driver both at night and during the day.
D   He was an expert gunman, both in terms of gun maintenance and shooting.
E   He was a seasoned pro at escaping, by shooting his way pass the law.
F   He was a seasoned pro at robberies.
G   Bonnie was a seasoned pro at promoting the gang.

End of Note

April 29, 1934
Bonnie writes in her diary that Clyde has received a large sum of cash as a

partial payment, to free a prominent prisoner. She makes no reference to who this prisoner is or what prison he was in.

April 9, 1934
Bonnie makes reference that she needs to deliver Sonny Boy, the rabbit, to her mother before he was captured or killed in another gunfight.

March 19, 1934
Bonnie makes reference to the fact that she was expecting a baby in the autumn.

March 8, 1934
Bonnie writes they now know who is hunting them down. He is Frank Hamer, the famous Texas Ranger. They know he has many kills to his name, and he prefers taking his prey dead.

February 25, 1934
Bonnie writes, she has tried again to convince Clyde that they are both going to die a terrible death if they don't change their ways. Clyde agrees, but he is unwilling to change.

February 14, 1934
In her diary, on this date, Bonnie writes she had a long talk with Clyde about their situation and that they are being hunted. Bonnie says straight out she fears for her life. Clyde was taking the news in stride.

February 5, 1934
At one of the stores, the gang robbed after leaving Shamrock, Texas; Bonnie wrote a short note about a funny event, which happened.

Clyde was holding a handgun on the store owner, who was the only one in the store at the time. The elderly man with his hands on the counter suspected the robbers were the Barrow Gang. The man took a high stakes gamble and blurted out your Bonnie and Clyde. Bonnie turned around and told him, yes, we are. The man then gambling further with his life by asking Bonnie if he could have his picture taken with them. He said no one was going to believe that Bonnie and Clyde robbed him.

Bonnie then told him, sure as long as you give us a camera and some film. The storekeeper agreed, and Bonnie asked Clyde to come over for the picture. Clyde immediately told Bonnie, we don't have time for this B.S., but Bonnie insisted telling Clyde, the storekeeper was giving us all these goods. Clyde mumbled something under his breath and walked over for the picture.

February 2, 1934
Bonnie writes her and Clyde have received information that Lee Simmons, the head of Eastham Prison, wants them dead. They are told Simmons has hired a Texas Ranger to hunt them down.

January 16, 1934
Bonnie writes in her diary about a successful raid on Eastham. She mentions Clyde is happy with the raid and wants to move on.

January 7, 1934

Bonnie writes today that she and Clyde have been lying low in a small cabin since just before Christmas. However, Clyde is starting to get worried about the calm period and they will be hitting the road tomorrow.

January 1, 1934

Bonnie writes that she and Clyde are feeling safe today, as Hamer would be home with his family. Bonnie says she was safe in a small cabin and they have wine, turkey, vegetables and apple pie for dessert.

Chapter 17
Whatever Happened To:

The Death Car

There is no doubt "The Death Car" as it has been coined was the most famous car in the world.

Description: 1934 Ford Model 730 Deluxe V-8 Sedan
Assembly Plant: River Rouge
Assembly Date: February 1934
Dealership: Mosley-Mack Motor Company
Engine: 85 HP V8
Transmission: Manual 3 speed
Tires: 525/550x17
Colour: Desert Sand (light tan)
Serial Number: 649198
Inside Options: Arvin hot water heater and fancy seat covers.
Outside Options: Front and rear bumper guards. Side windows that rolled up and down, and slid backward two inches for partial ventilation. Front and back doors swung outward towards the rear to open. Running boards were wide and curved. Spare tire had a metal cover over it. Radiator cap had a leaping greyhound attached to it in chrome. Safety glass windows, and Potters trunk.

Remarks: The Ford Motor Company said it would get 20 miles to the gallon at 45 mph and said its top speed was much faster.
Owner: Ruth Warren of Topeka, Kansas. Her husband, Jesse, was a roofing contractor.
Purchase Date: Mid March 1934
Purchase Price: $785.92 disagreement on the price.
Original License Plate Number: Kansas 3-17198 disagreement on the number
Date Stolen: April 29, 1934, from the Warren home in Topeka, Kansas.
Final License Plate on it: Arkansas 15-368
Miles added by Clyde: 2,500
Damage Assessment: Bullet holes and bloodstains.
General Remarks: Both husband and wife drove the car, but Ruth felt it was more hers than his. Jesse gave the dealership $200.00 down with the balance of $585.92 to be paid by April 15, 1934. By the end of April, the Warrens had paid the balance owing, and they had put 1298 miles on it.

In no time, the news service in the U.S. wired the ambush and the deaths of Bonnie and Clyde across the country. The news spread like wildfire. Duke Mills, a Kansas entrepreneur who specialized in displays, contacted

Jesse Warren. He had a plan to exhibit the car at the Chicago World's Fair. The deal was to pay $50 a week to rent the car and pay Jesse a commission on the take. After agreeing to the terms, Warren and a lawyer named Hall Smith went to Louisiana to get the car released. However, Sheriff Jordan refused to release it, stating it had to stay for evidence.

To make sure no one tried to steal the car, Jordan had it hidden, and only a couple of people knew where it was. Finally, Jesse Warren figured he would never be able to get the car back and gave up the issue. However, his wife Ruth was far from finished, and she travelled to Louisiana to get the car herself.

After arriving in Arcadia, Ruth went to see Jordan about getting the car back. Jordan told her she would have to pay $15,000 to get it back. She then went out and hired a respectable lawyer named W.D. Goff. This lawyer bypassed local jurisdiction and filed in Shreveport before U.S. Judge Ben Dawkins. The judge wasted no time in bringing Sheriff Jordan before him, and charged him with contempt of court, for refusing to release the car.

Ruth took possession of the car, which had been hidden in a barn in Arcadia. The story goes that Ruth made no bones about driving the blood and brain stained car back to Shreveport. She rented a van, and the car was put inside and taken back to Topeka. By this time, it was the beginning of August 1934, over two months since Bonnie and Clyde were killed.

Ruth had the car unloaded, and it was parked in her driveway. She hired a security company, which provided 24-hour security for the car. Ruth kept the car in her driveway until she signed a contract, leasing it to John Castle of United Shows. Her neighbours were horrified that she would leave such a disgraceful car on her property. The car was shot up, and the interior was a grizzly mess.

When Castle took over the car, he had it exhibited at the Topeka fairgrounds. For an admission, anyone could have a look inside it. In September 1934, Ruth went back to court to repossess the car as Castle defaulted on the rent payment. With the car returned to her, she rented it to Charles Stanley, a carnival man from Cleveland, for $200 a month.

From 1935 to 1940, it's unclear if Stanley had the car all that time. In 1940, Ruth sold the car to Charles Stanley for $3500. In 1952, Ted Toddy bought the car for $14,500. In 1973, the car was auctioned for $175,000. Whoever the buyer was, sold it in 1988 to Whiskey Pete's for $250,000.

The car was on display at the Gold Ranch Casino near Reno, Nevada, for a few years. Apparently, it is now on permanent display at the Primm Hotel and Casino in Primm, Nevada.

The Warren's new Ford Sedan in those thirty seconds of violence in 1934 went from ordinary to famous.

The Wellington Ford Car
That car likely went to the car wrecking yard in the sky. It was said;

someone from the general area removed the car from the riverbed, fixed it up and drove it. It seems the law was very relaxed in those days, and no big deal was made about the car.

Jones

Jones ran with Bonnie and Clyde for eight months, before leaving them. In 1935, he was sentenced to fifteen years in jail for his part in the crime spree. After Jones was released from prison, he never made anything of himself. He died in 1974 from gunshot wounds.

In later years, Jones did give an interview about his life with Bonnie and Clyde. In that interview, he said he never saw Bonnie pack or shoot a gun, and other gang members over the years testified to the same thing. Jones said the only time he saw Bonnie handle guns was for pictures, transferring them from one car to another or taking them into tourist court cabins. However, he did say she was an excellent re-loader.

Raymond Hamilton

Hamilton was executed in the electric chair on May 10, 1935, at the Texas State Penitentiary in Huntsville, Texas.

Joe Palmer

Palmer was executed on May 10, 1935, at the Texas State Penitentiary in Huntsville, Texas, by the electric chair.

Charles Baker

After the ambush, Baker resumed his life and career as a freelance photographer. In 1985, months before his death, he gave distant relatives information, which he had never revealed. The deal was to release that information in the year 2010.

Chapter 18
Is Bonnie Resting in Peace?

Bonnie and Clyde died in what most Americans believe was the most famous ambush in American History. The couple was taken back to Dallas and buried in separate cemetery's miles apart. Bonnie was buried in Crown Hill Memorial Park, 9700 Webb Chapel Road in North Dallas. In 2010, the cemetery had 1710 interments.

The killing of Bonnie and Clyde certainly captured the American interest, but over time, it faded, probably because of the Second World War. However, the ambush and the way they died did not entirely disappear. Even though they were dangerous outlaws, the circumstances of their deaths will probably always be questioned.

The posse of six lawmen who killed them acted without due process, and they were not given the opportunity to surrender. Even though Clyde vowed he would never be taken alive, the lawmen could have given him fair warning. After all, six lawmen were standing parallel with the car. At least two of them were eight feet away, with automatic rifles raised and ready to fire at point-blank range. Clyde may have been an expert shot, but there was no way he could have out-drawn them.

The posse played it safe and took Clyde out with the first shot. There was a debate as to whether this was by accident or planned. With Clyde dead, Bonnie was still alive, and these men should certainly have given her the opportunity to surrender. New information now suggests Bonnie was indeed trying to surrender. Apparently, she was still unhurt, pregnant and fully aware of the situation about her impending death. She was no threat to them and would have surrendered peacefully. However, that wasn't the plan. Hamer wanted them both dead.

It does seem a bit strange that they kept firing at the car, till they had over 150 rounds into it. Really, Bonnie had 50 hits on her body, while Clyde had thirty. Were these lawmen that scared, of B&C or were they trying to send a message. Either way, they managed to elevate the legends of these two outlaws, well into the stratosphere. Today, over three-quarters of a century later, the interest in these two outlaws, who lived and died by the gun, is growing into a tale of mythical proportions.

Bonnie was wildly popular when she died, and how it happened just elevated her aurora. Over a dozen brutal killings had severely tainted the rest of the Barrow gang's popularity. There were over 20,000 people at Bonnie's burial service. So many, that the family had trouble getting to her gravesite. At the time of her death, the American feeling was weighed heavily in her favour and even more so today.

Much of the American sentiment was focused on the dishonourable way in which Bonnie and Clyde died. There was a blatant disregard of the constitutional guarantees enshrined in the Fourth Amendment. The lawmen were well aware that Bonnie was not wanted for any capital offences. That does raise the question, was she murdered in cold blood?

Chapter 19
The Final Word
From the Great Grand-daughter of Charles Baker

As stated in this e-book, my great-grandfather was a photographer. Upon his death, the family discovered full disclosure from his writings and ambush notes. Frank Hamer promised Charles Baker full credit for his pictures and a write-up about the B&C ambush. However, the ambush did not go as planned, and because of that, Hamer threatened Baker, if he ever talked about the incident. Hamer confiscated all the film that Baker shot that morning, and that was how it ended.

About fifteen months later, Hamer got in touch with Baker. He apologized to him for his parting comments. Hamer's immediate concern was preserving the film and pictures of the ambush for a future release. He told Baker, he could not bring himself to destroy the film, but at the same time, he absolutely did not want it released anytime in the foreseeable future.

Baker though he was talking about 50 to 100 years down the road. As it turned out, Hamer was looking at 250 years into the future. He wanted several generations to die-off, thus creating in his words a buffer zone. Baker made a couple of suggestions, but he rejected them.

If they did not come to an agreement, Baker believed the pictures and video may never be released. The two men continued discussions, but Hamer was not very flexible. Baker then got the idea of releasing a book about B&C adventures, which would include a chapter about the real events surrounding the ambush. The book could be released on the 75th anniversary of the ambush. He told Hamer, the book would act as a gauge to measure the mood of the public.

Baker stated, if the book draws a negative response, then we will play it your way. However, if the book draws a favourable response, then all the film could be released on the 150th anniversary of the ambush. The public should have no problem with that, and it would be a feather in your cap for not destroying the valuable film. Hamer came back after a few days of mulling it over and agreed to the awkward compromise.

In summary, Baker would have a book released in the year 2010, describing the ambush. Baker wanted that particular year because it would coincide with Bonnie's last poem. Hamer did not know about that poem, or the circumstances surrounding it. The remaining B&C material would be released in the year 2084 if the public's disposition towards the book was favourable. If the public's mood towards the book was negative, then the balance of the material would be released in 2184.

The remaining material consists of Charles Baker's personal notes, the video and still pictures that were taken the morning of the ambush (no soundtrack). There is also the video (with sound) of a taped interview with Bonnie and Clyde.

The great grand-daughter followed the original book's release, and the mood was very negative. Her objective now is to follow the instructions that Charles Baker left. She will be passing these instructions down to future family members, and the organization that owns the time vault, where the material is being stored. She would like to emphasize at this time that all the film and notes have been stored in a climate-controlled time vault. As the technology evolved, the film was upgraded, and today a full digital copy of all the video film and still pictures are also in storage.

She also wants to point out that the original author only became aware of these details, after he agreed to a transfer of the book's rights. He is now under an agreement to keep his silence about what he has seen and heard.

Bateman wishes the outcome would have been different, so the material could have been released as planned. Frank Hamer made it very clear; there was no room for compromise. However, Bateman may have shown a hint of flexibility on the 2184 date. Her comments suggest she would like it released sooner than later.

Retribution 2015 Update

To satisfy a growing demand for the original Bonnie & Clyde book called Retribution, Mrs. Bateman has decided to re-release that book. It was originally written by her great grandfather Charles Baker. His instructions were very clear. He wanted the book released in 2010 with no changes to the manuscript. His instructions were carried out by the author that he chose in 1985, just a few months before his death.

The contract that Charles Baker and Frank Hamer agreed upon was airtight, and it left Baker with no room to maneuver. Back then, Hamer was holding all the cards, and it was either play ball my way or no way. Baker agreed to the rules to save the video and stills he took that day in 1934.

Bateman has stated, the likely reasons for the renewed interest in that book are centred around the following three items, the fact that the book was written by Charles Baker, who was with the posse when they killed Bonnie & Clyde in 1934, the latest B&C movie that came out in 2013, and an old newspaper article from that era, found in a scrapbook. The newspaper clipping states there was a photographer with the posse that morning.

At this time, Mrs. Bateman wants to clarify that her book, Decision at Ambush Hill, is almost an identical copy of the Retribution book. This updated Retribution book does contain new information about that morning in 1934. The book also includes information on when the family is going to release all the videos and still pictures. For the first time, Mrs. Bateman has announced exciting information about a new movie that will be centred on those hours before and during the ambush scene.

Movie / Documentary

These little people, who tried to suppress any new information about the Bonnie & Clyde ambush, did succeed in hurting her book sales at first. Then in 2013, with the release of the latest Bonnie & Clyde movie, all that changed. Sales for the book, Decision at Ambush Hill, took off, and even Bateman was caught off guard. Although the sales have come back down to Earth, the book is still selling at a respectable rate.

It was the sales from her book that convinced Bateman, making a movie centred on the actual ambush could prove to be a wise decision. The company that updated the video and stills that are in storage proved to be a valuable asset. That company had the latest high-tech equipment in real-life animation.

To show Mrs. Bateman how authentic human animation has evolved, the company made a three-minute movie showing human movement, close-up views of bullets hitting human flesh, human expression, laughter and speech. The company also included in the demo movie, vegetation, water, wind, smoke, and various sounds. Mrs. Bateman and several members of her family viewed the short movie and were in total awe at how real the video clip was.

The head engineer told them, with today's software, and employing meticulous detail, we can make it look authentic. After a few rounds of negotiations with the company, Mrs. Bateman and her family reached a deal with them. The agreement was to produce a 1.5 hour made for TV documentary movie in HD.

In the spring of 2015, one member of Mrs. Bateman's family, and one animation engineer from the company traveled to Louisiana. Their goal was to film that section of the road, where the ambush happened. They made notes and acquired samples of ground vegetation, trees, soil, insects, and gravel. The weather conditions were also noted in that area. The road scenery has changed over the years. However, from the information they gathered and old pictures of the city, they are confident the TV movie will look just as real as it did that morning in 1934.

The company has also purchased a scale model of the death car, various guns Clyde had with him and other items that were in the car. The pictures that Baker took of the car from every angle, inside and out, will let the crew reconstruct the bullet holes with accuracy. Anyone viewing this movie will need a strong stomach because the blood and flesh that was splattered around the inside of the car will also be created in living color. The company has acquired pictures of the posse members, Bonnie & Clyde, and Baker.

This company takes pride in its ability to restore videos and still pictures, along with creating life-like human animation. The company aggressively went after this project, knowing that they would never be able to purchase the kind of exposure and advertising they will be credited with. With their equipment, skills and training, the employees of that company are willing to take whatever time is necessary to come up with a movie documentary that will amaze and shock the public.

The Newspaper Article

In 2013, Mrs. Bateman received a newspaper article in the mail. It mentioned, there was a photographer with the posse. The newspaper clipping verifies, there was a seventh man with the posse. This latest development has lifted a weight off Bateman's shoulders. She now knows the name of the newspaper and the town where it was located. She did say I could release that information, but those little people think they are so self-righteous let them track it down.

Release Date, For The 1934 Video and Still Pictures

Mrs. Bateman has indicated the release date for the video and stills that Charles Baker took that morning in 1934 is May 23, 2184, exactly 250 years after it happened. Frank Hamer wanted several generations of those involved and their families to die off before the release.

The release date would have happened much sooner, except for the fact that the little people in this world, published hate literature aimed at the book and its author. That triggered a clause in the Hamer Baker agreement setting the release date back decades. It fits right in with the Bonnie & Clyde saga. They kept eluding the police, and so the video and stills will continue to elude those who want to see them most.

References

Running with Bonnie and Clyde
FBI Records and Information
Riding with Bonnie and Clyde
The Story of Suicide Sal
The Story of Bonnie and Clyde
Bonnie and Roy
Bonnie and Clyde's Texas Hideouts
Bonnie and Clyde's Revenge on Eastham
On the Trail of Bonnie and Clyde
Find a Grave
Red Crown Incident
Platte County Landmark
FBI famous cases: Bonnie and Clyde
Ambush: The Real Story of Bonnie and Clyde
Bonnie and Clyde Treasures
The Life and Times of Bonnie and Clyde
Dallas Morning News
Dallas Dispatch
Emma Parker's letters
Washington Times
In Search of Bonnie and Clyde in Louisiana
Baker Family Memories

Charles Baker's Notes
American Outlaws
American Folk Heroes
The Strange History of Bonnie and Clyde
The Texas Rangers
The Joplin Hideout
Dexfield
Was That Bonnie and Clyde
Bonnie and Clyde in Michigan
Bonnie and Clyde Vacation in Florida
The Buried Loot of Bonnie and Clyde
Famous Shootouts
Bonnie and Clyde Meet Jesse James
Outlaw Heaven

This Page is for notes

www.ingramcontent.com/pod-product-compliance
Lightning Source LLC
Chambersburg PA
CBHW062158290526
45791CB00016B/1158